There's More to Playing the Piano...

A thorough explanation of music theory
with practical keyboard activities
and video links for each topic

David Hall

Contents

Note Values • • • 4

Naming Notes • • • 7

Sharps and Flats • • • 9

Rests • • • 11

Bars and Bar lines • • • 13

Clefs • • • 16

Intervals (part 1) • • • 18

Key Signatures • • • 20

The Cycle of Fifths (part 1) • • • 22

Major Scales • • • 24

Chords • • • 26

Traffic Light Diagram • • • 28

The Cycle of Fifths (part 2) • • • 30

The Good Chords • • • 32

Chords and Cadences • • • 34

Ties and Dots • • • 38

Simple Time Signatures • • • 40

Compound Time Signatures • • • 42

Tuplets • • • 44

Switching Time Signatures • • • 46

Beaming • • • 49

Intervals (part 2) • • • 51

Minor Scales • • • 55

The Chromatic Scale • • • 58

Transposing • • • 60

Ornaments • • • 63

General Knowledge • • • 65

Style • • • 67

Musical Terms • • • 69

History of Music Theory • • • 83

ISBN 9798672771113
Copyright © 2020 David Hall. All rights reserved

About this book

Do you want to...

A – understand repertoire better, learn to improvise, compose, appreciate the skills and techniques of the great composers.

B – pass an exam.

They're both honourable aims and they are completely complementary.
If you absorb all the information in these pages and you try all the practical activities, you should end up with lots of new skills and you will be well on the way to passing the Grade 5 theory exam.

Unlike other theory textbooks, I have included a practical activity at the end of each chapter.

When you see this picture, try the activity at the piano. It will help you to understand the theory presented in the chapter and it will introduce you to some keyboard musicianship skills.

Scan the QR code at the start of each chapter to see a video demonstration of the keyboard activity and some further explanation of the theory topic. You can download a free QR code scanner to your phone or tablet at your app store.
QR Code is registered trademark of DENSO WAVE INCORPORATED.

1 Note Values

Most music has a steady beat.

The beat can be fast or slow depending on the piece of music being played. We describe our notes in terms of the beat, rather than trying to measure them in fractions of a second.

There are five very common notes that you will see in your music. Each of these notes has a different duration.

semibreve	minim	crotchet	quaver	semiquaver
𝅝	𝅗𝅥	♩	♪	𝅘𝅥𝅯
4 beats	2 beats	1 beat	½ beat	¼ beat

The diagram above assumes that one crotchet is one beat. This is a simplification - it is not always the case in pieces of music (see Chapter 17).

Each note can have a **note head**, a **stem** and a **tail**. Quavers and semiquavers can be joined together with **beams** (see Chapter 21).

4

A crotchet is typically one beat – but it is also known as a **quarter note**. This is because there are often four crotchets in each bar. You will often hear musicians counting 1-2-3-4, 1-2-3-4, 1-2-3-4 etc.

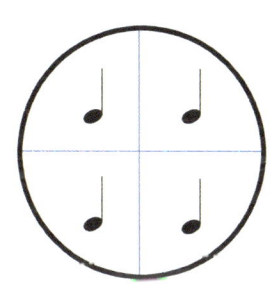

Similarly, a minim is also known as a **half note** because there are often two minims in each bar.

A semibreve is known as a **whole note** because there is often one semibreve filling the whole bar.

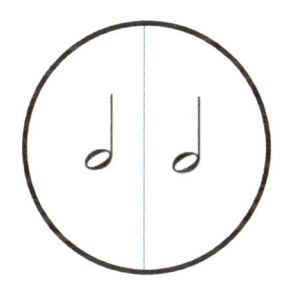

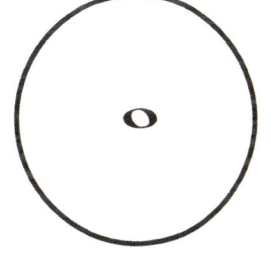

Quavers are known as **eighth notes**.

Semiquavers are known as **sixteenth notes**.

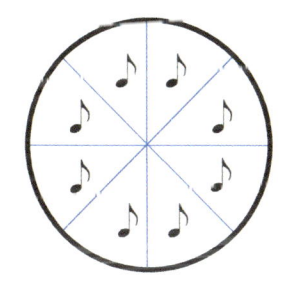

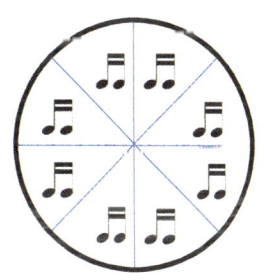

	British name	Duration (assuming ♩ = 1)	American name	Duration (compared to whole note)
𝅝	semibreve	4 beats	whole note	1
𝅗𝅥	minim	2 beats	half note	1/2
♩	crotchet	1 beat	quarter note	1/4
♪	quaver	1/2 beat	eighth note	1/8
𝅘𝅥𝅯	semiquaver	1/4 beat	sixteenth note	1/16

There are also longer notes called **breves** or **double whole-notes**. Each breve is twice the length of a semibreve.

There are also notes called **demisemiquavers** or **thirty-second notes**. Each demisemiquaver is half the length of a semiquaver.

There are also notes called **hemidemisemiquavers** or **sixty-fourth notes**. Each hemidemisemiquaver is half the length of a demisemiquaver.

At the piano

Stream some music or play some music on a CD or the radio. Play along in crotchets, then minims, then semibreves. Also, practise drawing these different notes.

2 Naming Notes

We describe squeaky notes as being high-pitched; we describe rumbly notes as being low-pitched. When we write music, we draw five lines – called the **stave** – and we place our notes high and low accordingly. Really high and really low notes are drawn on little extra lines called **ledger lines**.

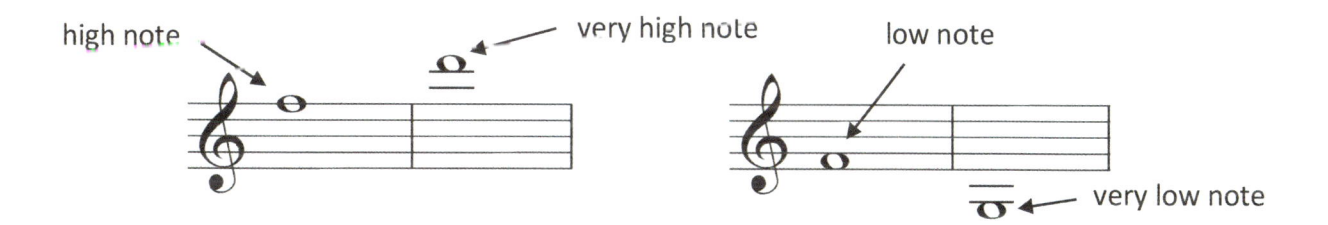

The notes that we use in music (A B C D E F and G) are written on the stave in simple alphabetical order.

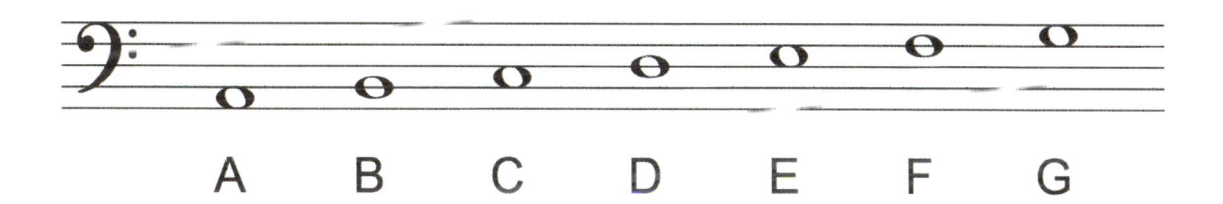

Most piano music is written on two staves. The right-hand part is written using the **treble clef** (see chapter 6). The left-hand part is written beneath using the **bass clef**.

The positions of the notes on the stave are slightly different in each clef. The following memory aids/mnemonics are helpful to speed up the learning process. These mnemonics are helpful but do not forget that the notes are, fundamentally, drawn in alphabetical order.

Notes of the treble clef:

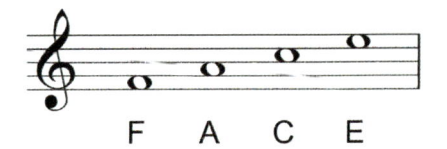

F A C E

Every Good Boy Deserves Football

Notes of the bass clef:

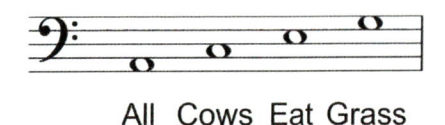

All Cows Eat Grass

Great Big Dogs From America

At the piano

Think of a tune that you know and write it out by hand. You could perhaps copy out part of a piano exam piece or you could try to write down something that you can play by ear.

3 Sharps and Flats

The black notes on the piano are often known as the **sharps** and **flats**.

This is a sharp sign - ♯. It indicates that you should play one semitone higher (sharper) than the printed note. One semitone higher is the very next note to the right on the piano.

This is a flat sign - ♭. It indicates that you should play one semitone lower (flatter) than the printed note. One semitone lower is the very next note to the left on the piano.

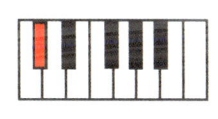

This is a **natural** sign - ♮. It indicates that you should play the white note on the piano. The natural sign is used only when necessary to cancel a sharp or flat sign.

Sharps and flats are often printed at the very start of a piece of music. These sharps and flats are known as **key signatures** (see Chapter 8).

Other sharps, flats and naturals that occur during the course of a piece of music are known as **accidentals**. They affect a note for the duration of a bar. Accidentals act only on the note they are drawn next to, not notes that are an octave higher or lower.

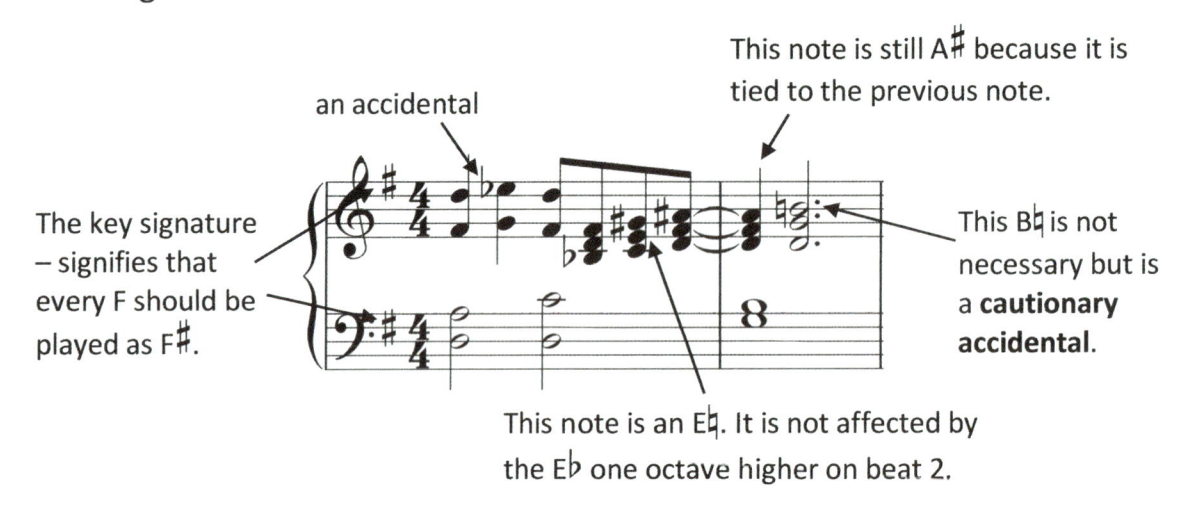

The key signature – signifies that every F should be played as F♯.

an accidental

This note is still A♯ because it is tied to the previous note.

This B♮ is not necessary but is a **cautionary accidental**.

This note is an E♮. It is not affected by the E♭ one octave higher on beat 2.

There are also **double sharps** x and **double flats** ♭♭ which raise or lower notes by two semitones.

G x is an **enharmonic equivalent** of A. That means that the two notes sound the same but are spelt differently. A♭♭ is an enharmonic equivalent of G.

At the piano

There are several tunes that we call "Chopsticks". At least two of them are played primarily on the black notes of the piano. Try to find a friend who can show you how to play Chopsticks.

4 Rests

A **rest** is a moment of silence. Every note value has its equivalent rest.

Note Name	Note	Rest
Breve Double Whole-note	𝄺	
Semibreve Whole note	𝅝	
Minim Half note	𝅗𝅥	
Crotchet Quarter note	♩	𝄽
Quaver Eighth note	♪	𝄾
Semiquaver Sixteenth note	𝅘𝅥𝅯	𝄿
Demisemiquaver Thirty-second note	𝅘𝅥𝅰	𝅀
Hemidemisemiquaver Sixty-fourth note	𝅘𝅥𝅱	𝅁

Rests can be dotted in the same manner as normal notes (see Chapter 16). Rests cannot be tied together.

In this example, notice how the rests are drawn so that each beat of the music is still clear.

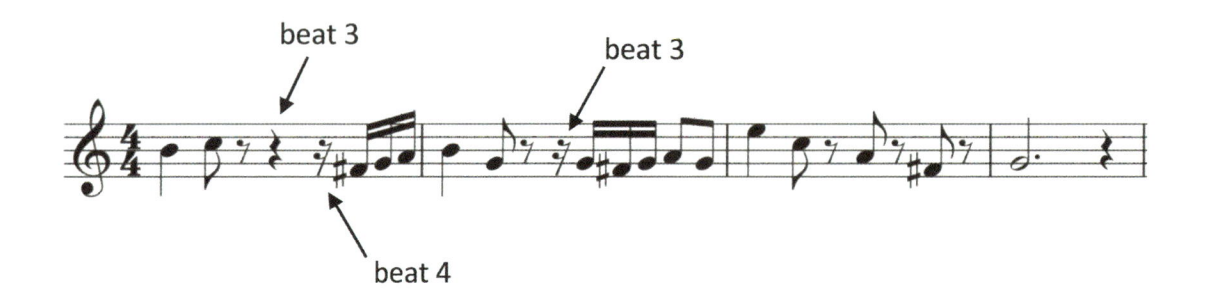

The semibreve rest can be used to indicate a full bar's rest regardless of the time signature. (see Chapter 17)

This symbol is known as a multirest -

It is rarely found in piano music, but is very familiar to orchestral musicians. This particular multirest indicates four bars of silence.

At the piano

Play through a piece that you know well. Whenever there are rests, listen closely to the silence. Many performers consider the rests to be more emotionally charged than the notes.

5 Bars and Bar lines

Music is divided into **bars** which usually comprise two, three or four beats. Each of these bars is separated by a **bar line**.

The first beat of each bar is usually played slightly more loudly than the subsequent beats and is called the downbeat. The last beat of each bar is known as the upbeat. These terms refer to conductors' gestures.

If there is a fragment of melody before the first bar line, it is known as an anacrusis. An anacrusis can be longer or shorter than the upbeat.

At the end of a section of music, you may find a **double bar line.** At the end of a piece you will find a **final bar line**.

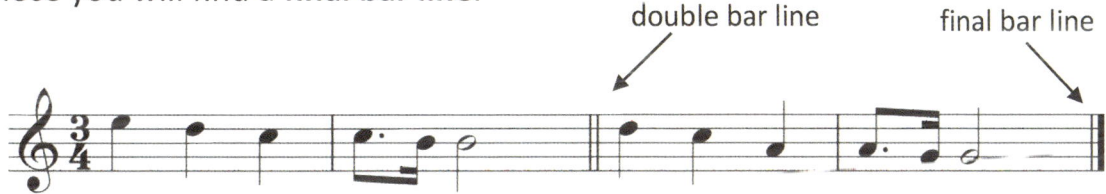

The two symbols below are known as **repeat marks**. The section of music that is printed between the two repeat marks should be repeated.

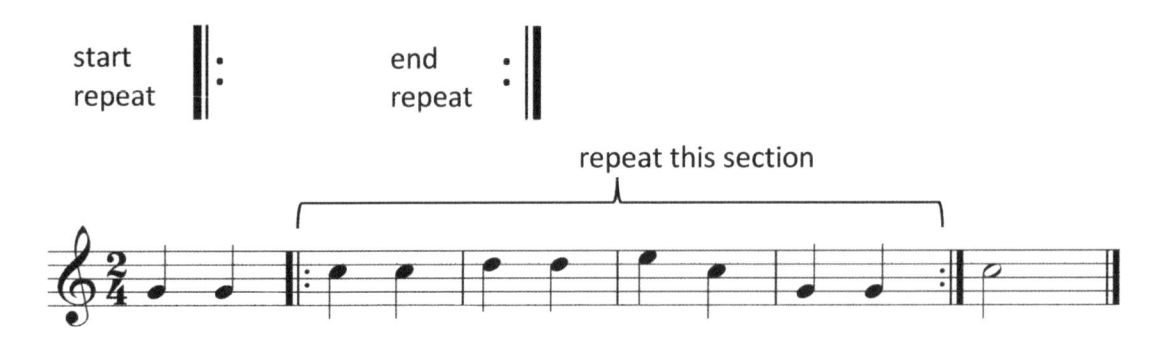

Sometimes the first repeat mark is omitted; in this case, repeat from the start of the piece.

A repeated section of music may end with bracketed passages that are labelled as 1. and 2. These are known as **first-time bars** and **second-time bars**. We tend to call them this even if the passages are several bars long.

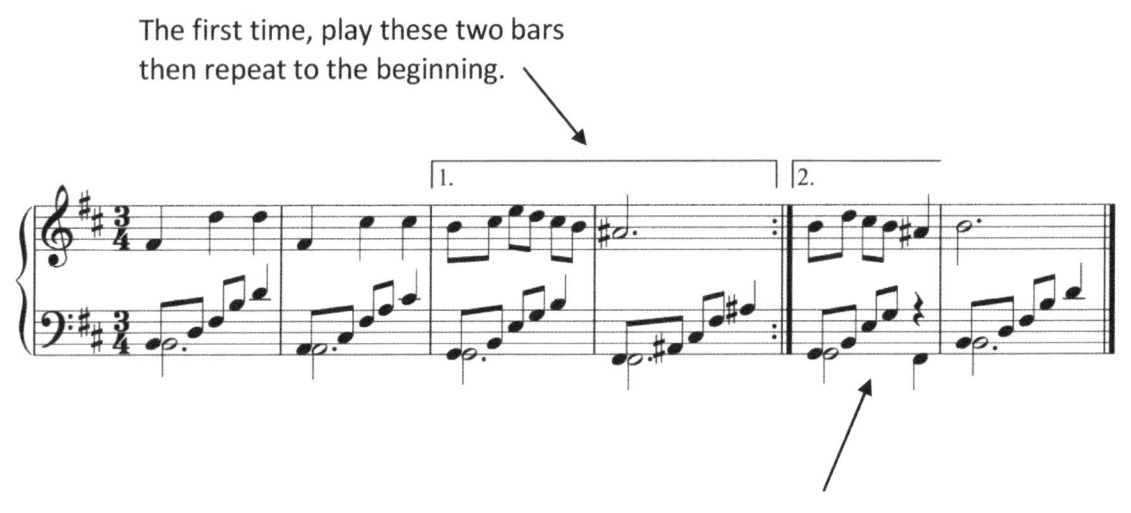

The instruction **DC** is an abbreviation of **Da Capo**. It means that you should repeat from the beginning of the piece until there is a further written instruction.

The instruction **DS** is an abbreviation of **Dal Segno**. It means that you should repeat from the sign 𝄋

There will then follow an instruction **fine** or **al coda**. **Fine** means that you have now reached the end of the piece. **Al coda** means that you should go to the coda (ending). This sign ⊕ will be printed alongside the **al coda** instruction and will also be printed at the start of the coda.

This symbol ∕. means that you should repeat the previous bar. It is used a lot in pop, jazz and stage music.

You may occasionally see the instruction "vamp till ready" or "repeat ad lib". This is common in music written for the theatre. It means that you should repeat the passage indefinitely while you wait for a cue from the stage or from the conductor.

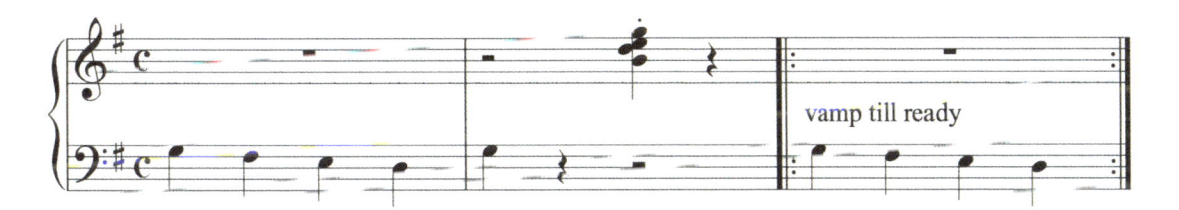

At the piano

Find a short piece that you know well (perhaps 16 bars long). Repeat it several times, changing the dynamic, the articulation, maybe even the texture.

6 Clefs

Clefs tell us exactly where the notes are written on the stave.

𝄞 is a G-clef. The symbol evolved from a lower case g to what we now know as the **treble clef**. The spiral is drawn starting on G.

𝄢 is an F-clef. The symbol evolved from a lower case f to what we now know as the **bass clef**. The two dots are drawn either side of F.

𝄡 is a C-clef. The symbol evolved from a lower case c to what we now know as the **alto clef** or **tenor clef**. The clef can be drawn centred on the middle line of the stave (alto) or one line higher (tenor). The clef is centred on C.

The word treble suggests a high range of notes; the word bass suggests a lower range of notes; alto and tenor fall in the middle.

The diagram opposite shows the position of middle C drawn in each clef. Middle C is the name commonly given to the C that lies in the middle of the piano range.

treble clef — middle C

alto clef — middle C

tenor clef — middle C

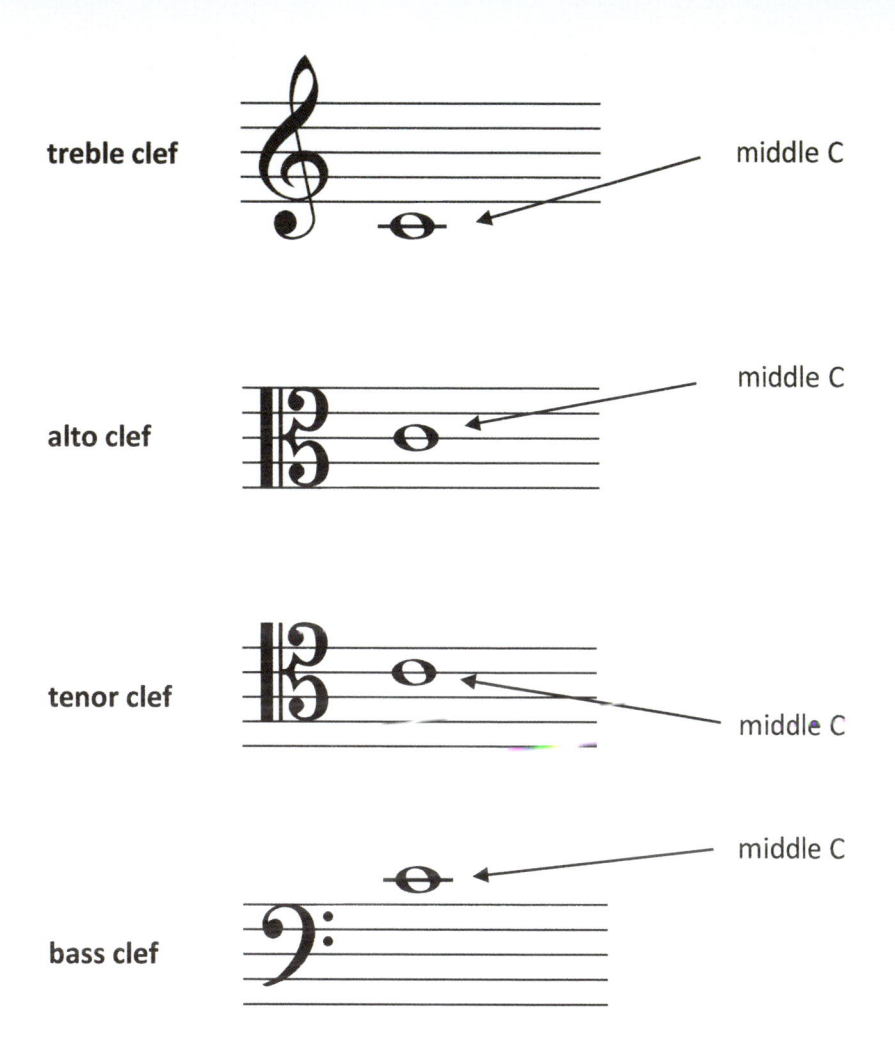

bass clef — middle C

Clefs are drawn at the very start of a piece of music, followed by the key signature (see Chapter 8) and then the time signature (see Chapter 17).

Remember the order by thinking of the word cricket.
Cricket ⟶ C---K-T ⟶ Clef – Key – Time.

At the piano
Download Haydn's string quartets opus 1 which are written with all three types of clef. Try to play the viola line which is written in the alto clef. Maybe even try to play the whole texture.

7 Intervals (part 1)

An **interval** is the distance from one note to another. The smallest interval that can be played on the piano is known as a **semitone** (e.g. C→C♯).
The distance of two semitones (e.g. C→D) is a **tone**.

If you play the first note of a scale and also play the second note, we say that you are playing a **second**.

If you play the first note of a scale and also play the third note, we say that you are playing a **third**.

We calculate intervals by counting the position of the notes on the stave or by counting letter names. At this stage, we disregard any sharps and flats.

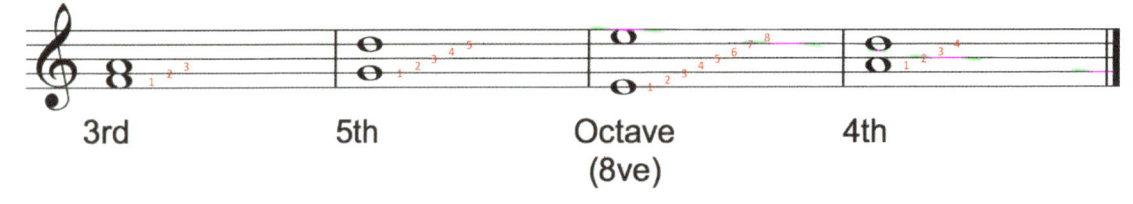

3rd   5th   Octave (8ve)   4th

Unisons, 4ths, 5ths and Octaves sound strong and bold.
3rds and 6ths are consonances (they sound nice).
2nds and 7ths are dissonances (they sound nasty).

When two or more instruments play the same note simultaneously, we say that they are playing in **unison**.

The music printed below demonstrates Parallel Thirds. The two voices are moving in parallel motion with a fixed interval of a third. This should sound nice (consonant) and is key to understanding chords and harmony.

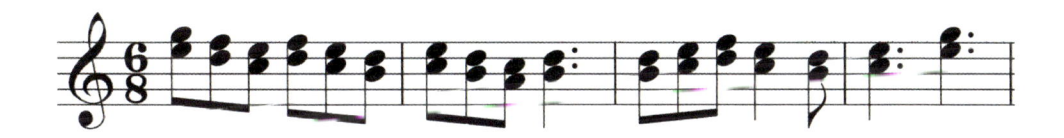

This next example demonstrates Parallel Seconds. The two voices are moving in parallel motion with a fixed interval of a second. This should sound nasty (dissonant). Composers use dissonance to create tension, pain, excitement and drama in their music.

When two notes are played together, they create a **harmonic interval**. When two notes are played consecutively, they create a **melodic interval**.

At the piano
Play several different intervals. Notice how each interval has a particular sonority and character. Improvise a melody using parallel thirds or fifths to appreciate these sonorities fully.

8 Key Signatures

The sharps and flats that are drawn at the start of every line of music are known as **key signatures**.

Key signatures tell us which sharps and flats to play throughout the piece. The sharps and flats in key signatures are written in a particular order.

The order is F C G D A E B for sharps.
The mnemonic **F**ather **C**hristmas **G**ave **D**ad **A**n **E**lectric **B**lanket is helpful.

♯ **F C G D A E B**

The order is B E A D G C F for flats.
The equivalent mnemonic is **B**lanket **E**xploded **A**nd **D**ad **G**ot **C**old **F**eet.

♭ **B E A D G C F**

This order of sharps and flats applies to both major and minor keys.

You will notice that the key signatures circled in red make perfect, satisfying zig-zag shapes. The remaining key signatures have a slight discrepancy in the placing of the fifth sharp (circled in blue). This disrupts the zig-zag pattern a little. This is a convention that helps to avoid drawing sharps up on ledger lines.

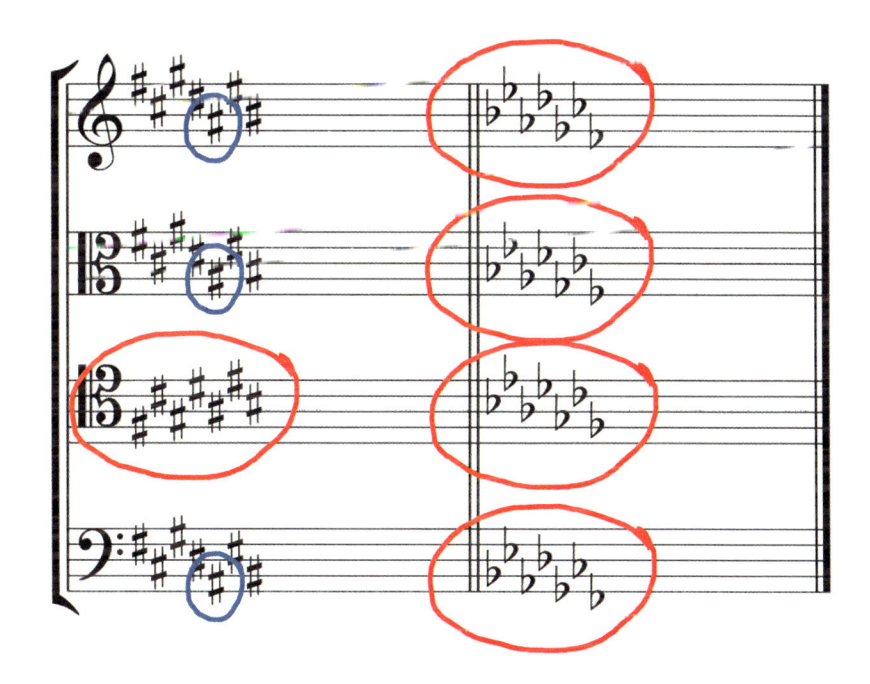

At the piano

Look at the key signatures in the music that you are learning. Notice that they follow the patterns outlined in this chapter. If you are able, play some of the "Well-Tempered Clavier" by JS Bach.

9 The Cycle of Fifths (part 1)

The **Cycle of Fifths** is the diagram that can most easily unlock the secrets of scales, arpeggios, chords, keys, key relationships and harmony. Each note on the Cycle of Fifths diagram forms the interval of a 5th with its neighbour.

Follow these steps to construct the diagram:

- Draw a neat circle
- Put a tiny pencil mark at the top, bottom, right and left (north, south, east and west).
- Put two further pencil marks in each quarter to create a clock face.
- Draw 0 in the top position (12 o'clock). Then label the diagram with the numbers 1 – 6 as if it were a clock.
- Now write 1 – 5 in the positions coming down anticlockwise to create a mirror image.
- Starting at the 11 o'clock position, mark in the keys F C G D A E B using the mnemonic **F**ather **C**hristmas **G**ave **D**ad **A**n **E**lectric **B**lanket.
- Starting at the 10 o'clock position, mark in B♭ E♭ A♭ D♭ G♭ using the mnemonic **B**lanket **E**xploded **A**nd **D**ad **G**ot (Cold Feet)
- Also add F♯ at the 6 o'clock position. F♯ and G♭ are known as **enharmonic equivalents** (same note - different spelling).

This simple version of the Cycle of Fifths shows how many sharps or flats are needed in each **major** scale, for example:

A is labelled with a 3, so A major scale needs three sharps.
B♭ is labelled with a 2, so B♭ major scale needs two flats.

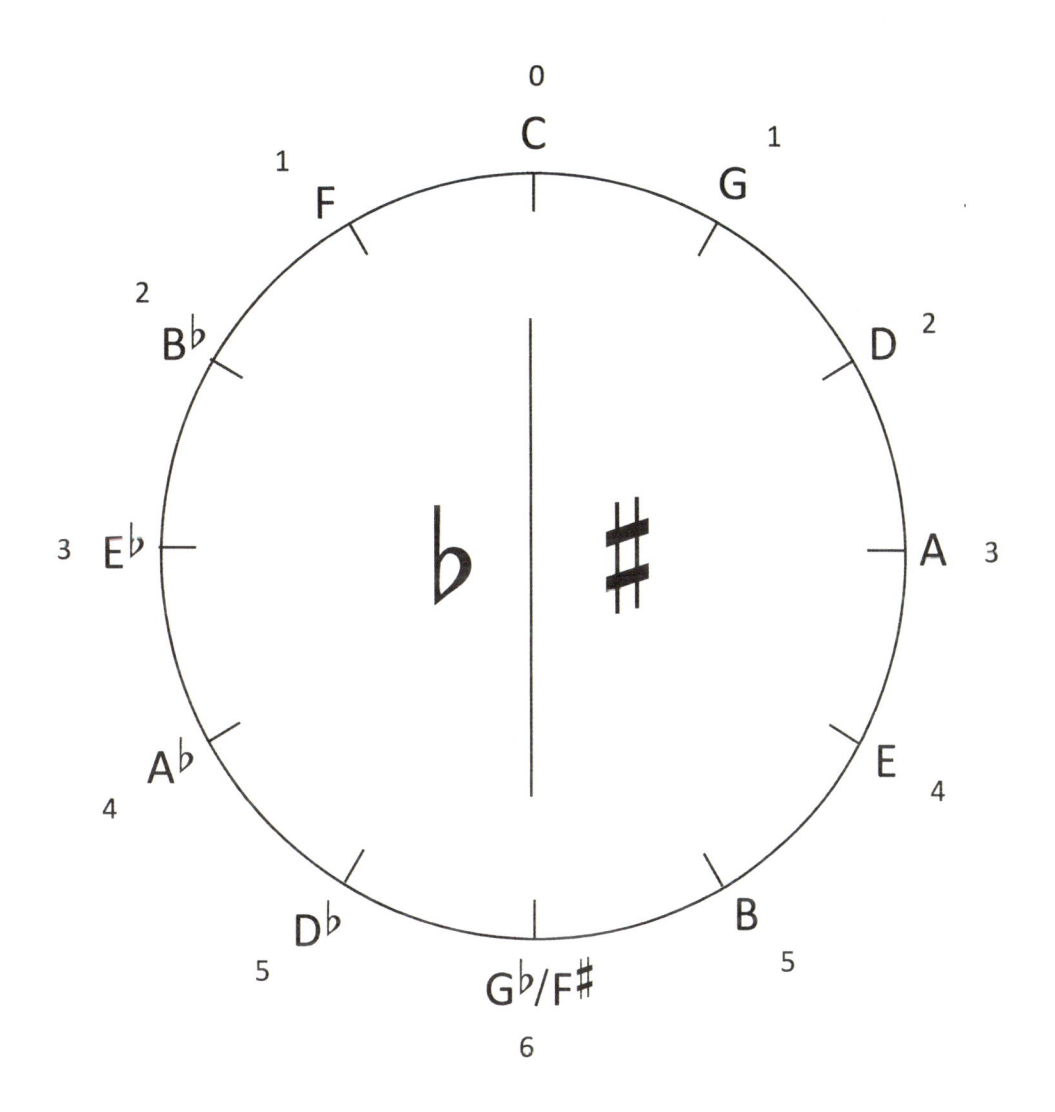

At the piano

Starting at C, play each note of the Cycle of Fifths travelling around anticlockwise (C, F, B♭, E♭ etc.). Now take a fragment of melody, perhaps C B C, on a journey around the Cycle of Fifths.

10 Major Scales

A **major scale** is a series of eight notes in alphabetical order that adheres to the necessary key signature.

C major is in position 0 of the Cycle of Fifths. It has 0 sharps and 0 flats.

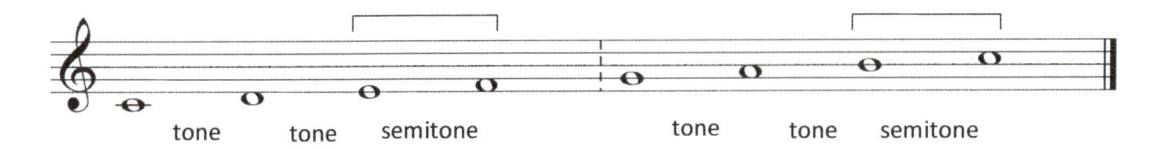

tone   tone   semitone   tone   tone   semitone

A major is in position 3 of the Cycle of Fifths. It has 3 sharps - F♯, C♯ and G♯.

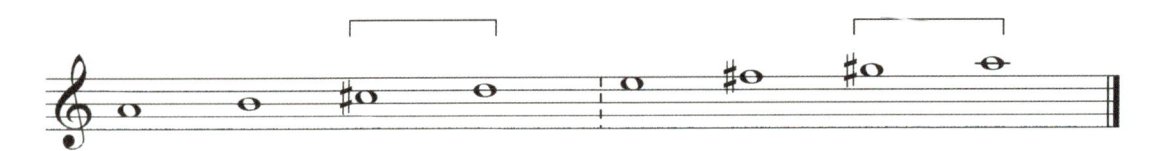

B♭ major is in position 2 on the flat side of the Cycle of Fifths. It has two flats - B♭ and E♭.

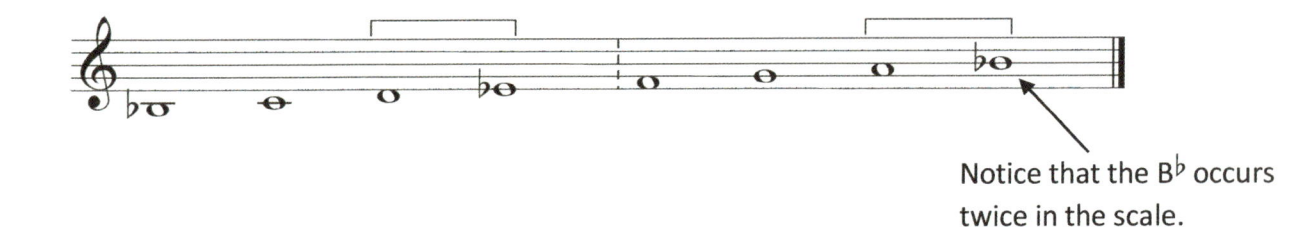

Notice that the B♭ occurs twice in the scale.

Every major scale has a characteristic pattern of tones and semitones. Looking at C major above, C→D is a tone; D→E is a tone; E→F is a semitone.
The brackets indicate the positions of the semitones.

Each major scale divides nicely into two halves (indicated by the dotted bar line). The first half of the scale ends with a semitone; the second half of the scale ends with a semitone.

It is this characteristic pattern of tones and semitones that gives each major scale its bright, major sound.

To construct a major scale:

- Check the clef that you are using.
- Draw eight consecutive notes starting with the first note of your scale (the tonic).
- Look at the Cycle of Fifths to find out how many sharps or flats are necessary.
- If the scale needs sharps, use the mnemonic **F**ather **C**hristmas **G**ave **D**ad **A**n **E**lectric **B**lanket to determine which sharps.
- If the scale needs flats, use the mnemonic **B**lanket **E**xploded **A**nd **D**ad **G**ot **C**old **F**eet to determine which flats.
- Draw the sharps and flats next to the applicable notes or as a key signature.
- Check the resulting pattern of tones and semitones.

At the piano

Play one octave of each major scale. Start with C major and then proceed clockwise or anticlockwise around the Cycle of Fifths. You should notice the similarities between adjacent scales.

11 Chords

A **chord** is any collection of notes played simultaneously. Some chords sound great, some less so.

The best chords to get to know first are **major** and **minor** chords in **root position**. Sometimes described as $\frac{5}{3}$ chords, these chords comprise the notes 1, 3 and 5 from the scale.

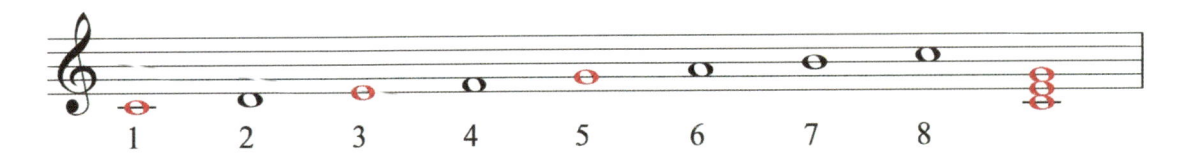

It is easy to spot a $\frac{5}{3}$ chord drawn on the stave because it will either be drawn on three consecutive spaces or on three consecutive lines.

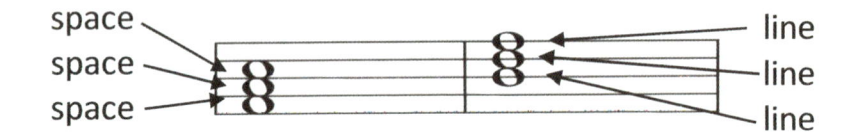

Major chords often contain sharps or flats and ought to be memorised, along with major scales. Chapter 12 will help you to memorise major chords.

The chords drawn in the example below are all chords of C major - they all have the notes C, E and G. The notes can be played at any octave and in any position. In each of these examples, the lowest note (in the bass clef) is C, so we say that they are in **root position**.

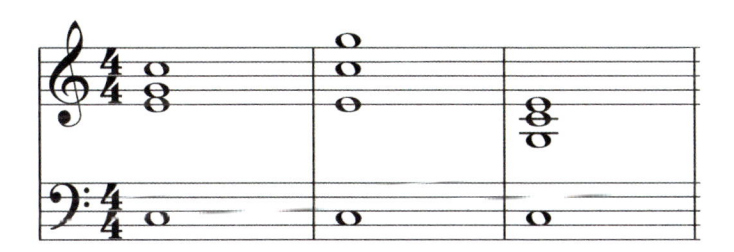

The chords drawn in this next example are not in root position because the **bass note** has changed. They are all chords of C major, but we treat them slightly differently and we give them different names (see Chapter 15). They are **inversions** of the chord.

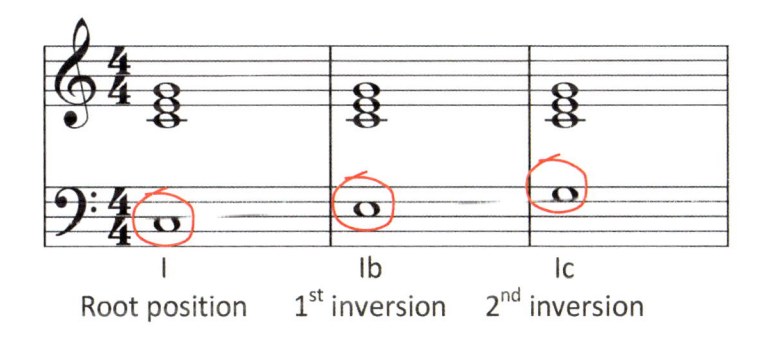

I
Root position

Ib
1st inversion

Ic
2nd inversion

At the piano

Improvise a piece of music using just one chord. There are endless possibilities to create atmosphere using texture, rhythms, dynamics etc.

12 Traffic Light Diagram

The traffic light diagram is not an essential diagram for understanding music theory. But it is a useful shortcut for learning every major chord shape on the piano.

○ denotes a white note.

● denotes a black note.

It is not necessary to draw a separate diagram for minor chords.

To create a minor chord, simply flatten the middle note of the chord (known as the third); for example, C major (C E G) becomes C minor (C E♭ G)

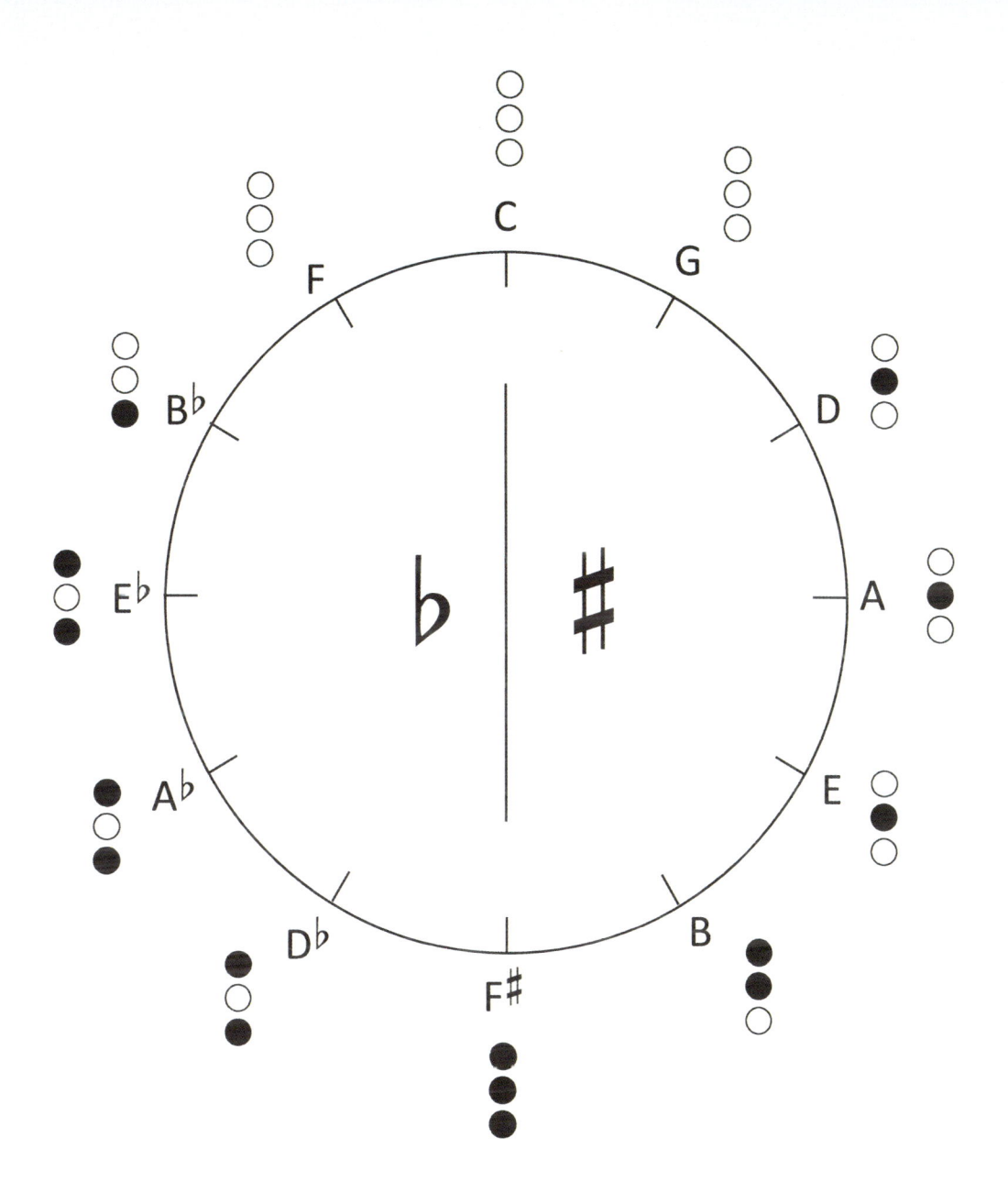

At the piano

Play all the chords. Start at C and then move anticlockwise around the Cycle of Fifths. Now play three-note arpeggios (broken chords) in the same way. Experiment with other ideas.

13 The Cycle of Fifths (part 2)

The Cycle of Fifths can be extended to include all the minor key signatures.

Each major key has a **relative minor** key that shares the same key signature.

For example, to find the minor scale with three flats:

- Look at the Cycle of Fifths diagram (see Chapter 9).
- E♭ major has three flats.
- Write out E♭ major scale – or play it on the piano.
- Count 3 notes down from the top of E♭ major scale to the note that we call the **submediant** - C.
- The relative minor of E♭ major is C minor. C minor has three flats.

Similarly, to find the relative minor of B major:

- Look at the Cycle of Fifths diagram (see Chapter 9).
- B major has five sharps.
- Write out B major scale – or play it on the piano.
- Count 3 notes down from the top of B major scale to the note that we call the submediant - G♯.
- The relative minor of B major is G♯ minor. G♯ minor has five sharps.

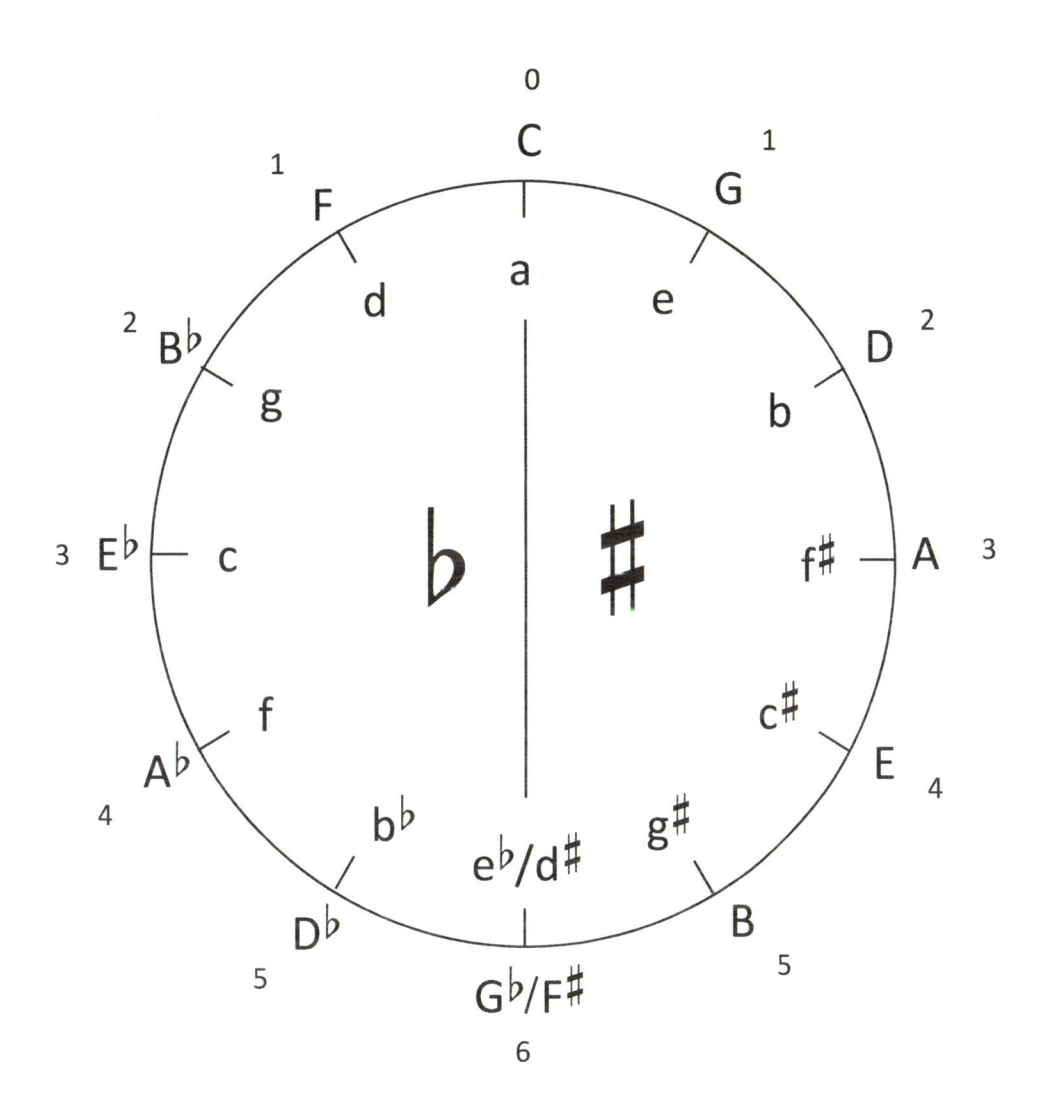

At the piano

Improvise some patterns and textures using major chords and their relative minor chords.

14 The Good Chords

As well as being a reference tool for key signatures and scales, the Cycle of Fifths is also a great way to understand chord relationships (**harmony**).

The last chapter mentioned relative major and minor chords. The other closely related chords are the **dominant** (clockwise around the cycle) and the **subdominant** (anticlockwise round the cycle)

In the key of C:

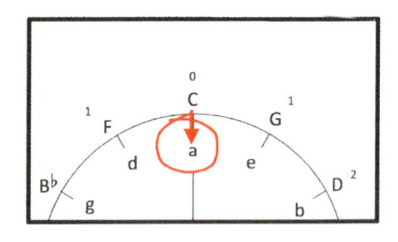

relative minor = a   dominant = G   subdominant = F

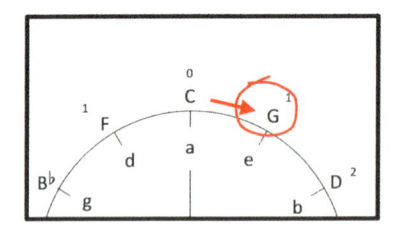

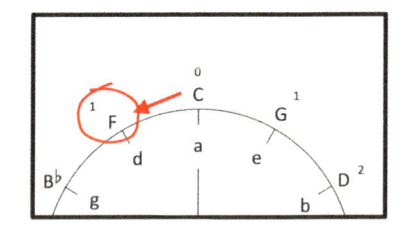

In the key of Am:

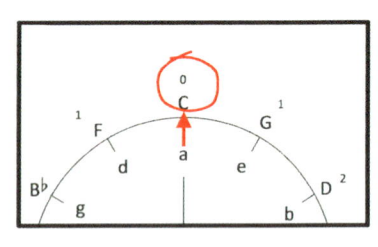

relative major = C   dominant = E*   subdominant = d

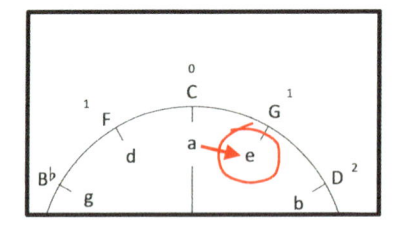

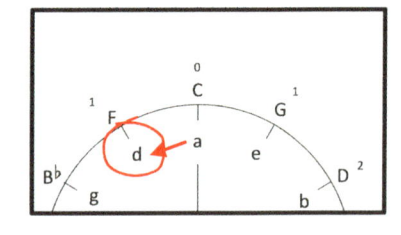

32

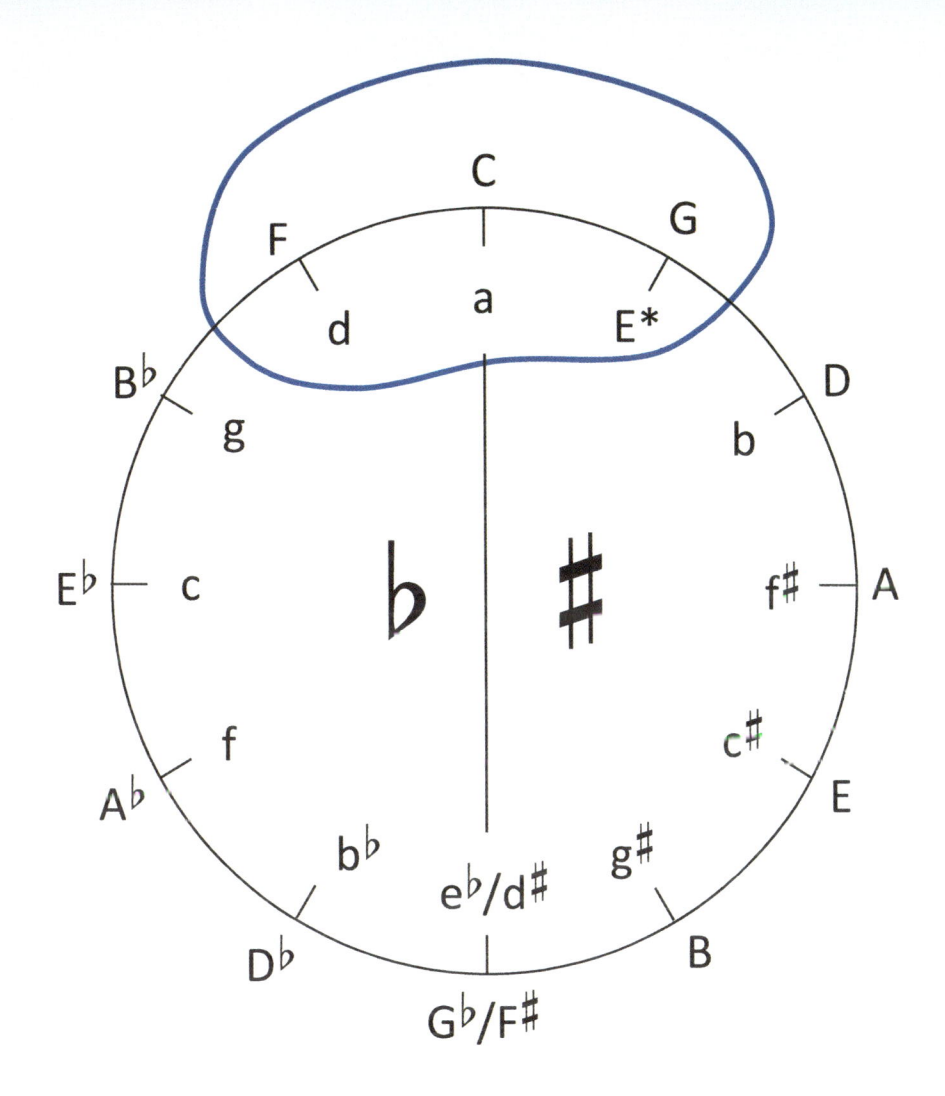

* In the key of A minor, we tweak the dominant chord from E minor (E G B) to E major (E G# B). This ties in with the **harmonic minor scale** (see Chapter 23).

At the piano

Make up a piece using the six chords that are circled. Move quite freely between one chord and another, but use the chord progressions G → C and E → Am most often.

15 Chords and Cadences

Another way to visualise related chords is in a Chord Table. Chord Tables help us to name chords and their inversions (see Chapter 11).

It is useful to know the technical names of the degrees of the major scale:

8 - tonic
7 – leading note
6 - submediant
5 - dominant
4 - subdominant
3 - mediant
2 - supertonic
1 - tonic

Chord Tables can be drawn in any key, with the **tonic** note in the bottom left-hand corner. Reading from the bottom upwards, the chord based on the tonic is called Chord I. Moving across, the chord based on the **supertonic** is called Chord ii etc. We use Roman numerals when describing chords – upper case for major chords; lower case for minor chords.

The chord tables on the next page show chords I, ii, IV and V (note that chord iii is omitted). These are the chords that are used most frequently and they are the chords most often encountered in theory exams.

A chord table can be read like a graph focussing on the bass note; for example, the chord – E♭, G, B♭ with G in the bass – would be called Ib.

Chord Table in the key of E♭ major

c	B♭	C	E♭	F
b	(G)	A♭	C	D
a	E♭	F	A♭	B♭
	I	ii	IV	V

This chord is printed in the key of E♭ major. The notes of the chord are E♭, G and B♭. The lowest note is the G in the bass - so this is chord Ib.

Chord Table in the key of A minor

c	E	F	A	B
b	C	D	F	G♯
a	A	(B)	D	E
	I	ii	IV	V

This chord is printed in the key of A minor. The notes of the chord are B D and F. The lowest note is the B in the bass - so this is chord ii.

Most music is constructed from **phrases** – often four-bars long – each of which ends with a "breath" in the melody.

The last two chords of each phrase are known as the **cadence**.

Imperfect Cadence	? → V	Sounds like a comma
Perfect Cadence	V → I	Sounds like a full stop
Plagal Cadence	IV → I	Sounds like an "Amen" / sounds bluesy
Interrupted Cadence	V → vi	Sounds like an exclamation mark

The **Imperfect Cadence** sounds like a quick breath, a comma, but does not sound like the end of the melody. The melody note will not be the tonic.
The first chord of the Imperfect Cadence can be I, ii or IV. The second chord is always V.

The **Perfect Cadence** sounds like a full stop, the end of the melody. The final melody note will often be the tonic but can be any note from chord I.
The first chord of the Perfect Cadence is V. The second chord is I.

The **Plagal Cadence** also sounds like a full stop, the end of the melody. Again, the final melody note will often be the tonic. The plagal cadence is used for choral "Amens" at the ends of hymns and – perhaps stemming from this – it is used as the main cadence in the blues. The two chords are IV then I.

The **Interrupted Cadence** occurs at a point in the melody where you might expect a Perfect Cadence. The preparation is chord V, then the music takes an unexpected twist to chord vi – the relative minor chord. Or – if the piece is in a minor key already – chord VI will be unexpectedly major.

Music **modulates** (changes key) frequently without the composer changing the printed key signature. To work out the key of a passage of music, look at all of the notes in the passage and consider what scale they belong to. Then look for a **perfect cadence** in that key.

The extract printed below is in the key of G major.

c	D	E	G	A
b	B	C	E	F#
a	G	A	C	D
I	ii	IV	V

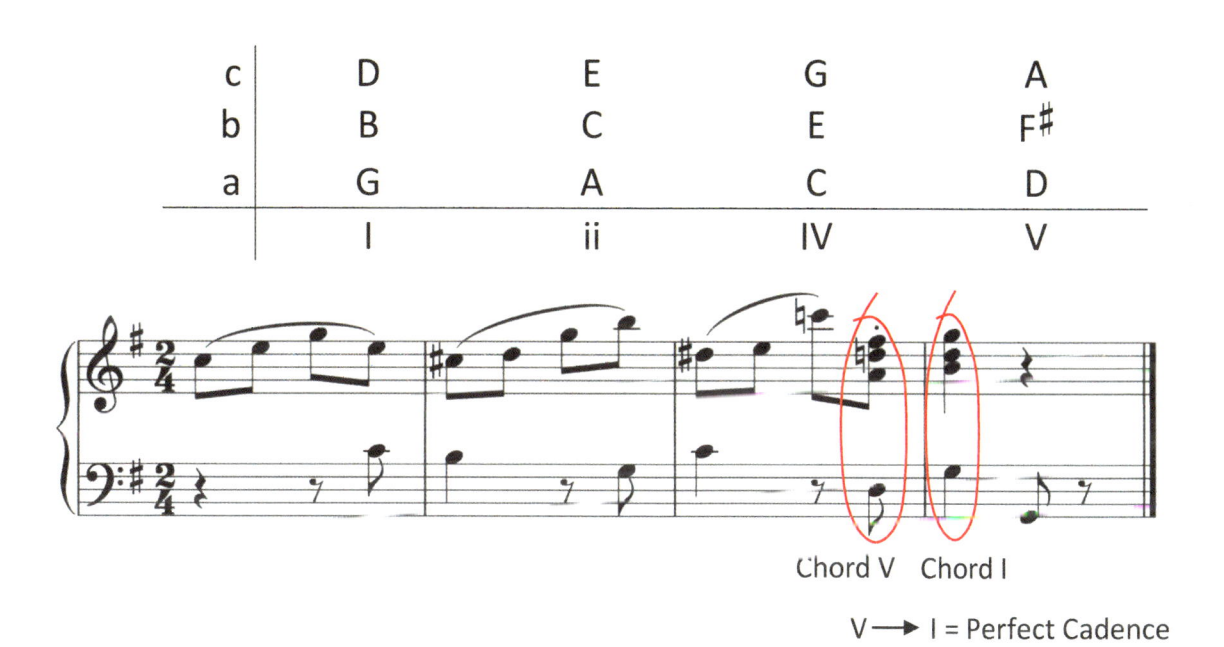

Chord V Chord I

V ⟶ I = Perfect Cadence

The extract printed below is in the key of A♭ major.

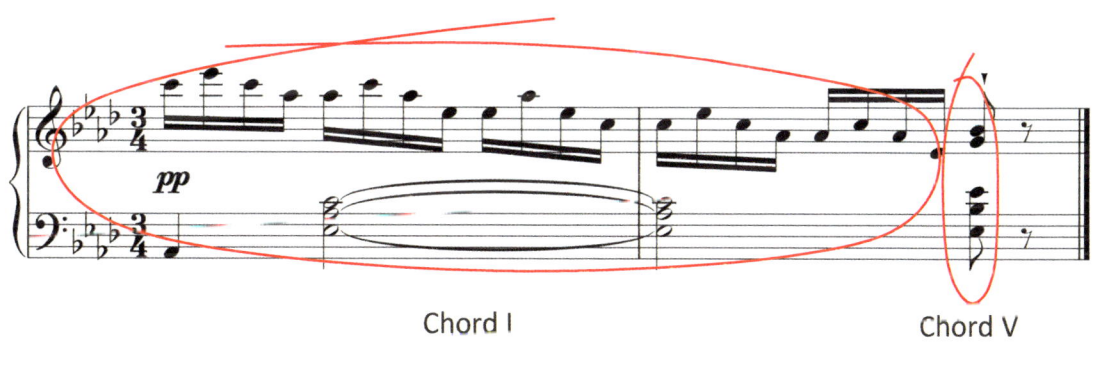

Chord I   Chord V

I ⟶ V = Imperfect Cadence

At the piano

Look through a piece you know. Work out what the chords and identify each of the cadences. This is the basis of musical analysis and should inform your performance of the piece.

16 Ties and Dots

Dots – not to be confused with staccato marks – make notes longer by 50%.

A crotchet ♩ = 1 beat   a **dotted crotchet** ♩. = 1½ beats.

A minim 𝅗𝅥 = 2 beats   a **dotted minim** 𝅗𝅥. = 3 beats.

Rests can also be dotted.

A double dot adds a further 25% to the duration of the note, so a double-dotted crotchet is worth 1¾ beats.

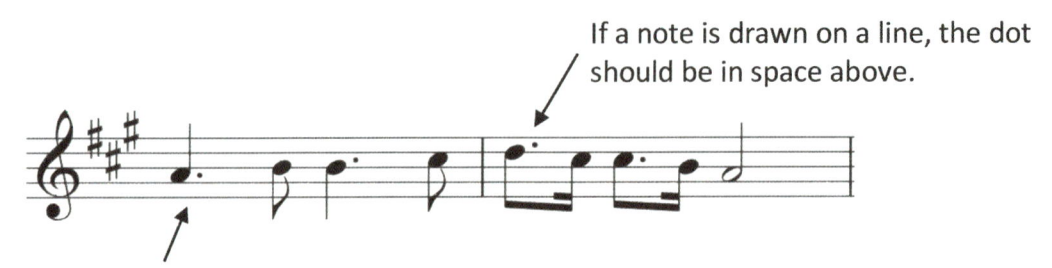

If a note is drawn on a line, the dot should be in space above.

If a note is drawn in a space, the dot should be in the same space.

Ties are used when a dot is impractical e.g. over a bar line, or when an unusual note length is required e.g. a minim tied to a quaver to make a note of 2¼ beats.

You may find that a note with an accidental is tied over a bar line. The accidental holds true for the duration of the tied note, but then no longer applies in the new bar.

♪.	= ¾ =	♪♬
♩.	= 1½ =	♩♪ (tied)
𝅗𝅥.	= 3 =	𝅗𝅥 ♩ (tied)
𝅝.	= 6 =	𝅝 𝅗𝅥 (tied)
♪..	= ⁷⁄₈ =	♪♬𝅘𝅥𝅰
♩..	= 1¾ =	♩♪♬ (tied)
𝅗𝅥..	= 3½ =	𝅗𝅥 ♩ ♪ (tied)
𝅝..	= 7 =	𝅝 𝅗𝅥 ♩ (tied)

At the piano

Find a tricky bit of passagework in one of your pieces. Practise it with a dotted rhythm and you will find that your fingers get stronger and more secure.

17 Simple Time Signatures

The top number of the **time signature** tells you how many beats there are in each bar.

The bottom number tells you what note value (crotchet, quaver etc.) corresponds to one beat. This bottom number is derived from the alternative note names (quarter note, eighth note etc.) described on page 5.

$\frac{3}{4}$ = 3 ♩ = 3 crotchets in each bar $\frac{2}{2}$ = 2 ♩ = 2 minims in each bar

$\frac{4}{4}$ - a **simple** time signature - has four crotchet beats in each bar. Each of those beats can be sub-divided into two quavers.

Count each bar like this: 1-and 2-and 3-and 4-and

Simple – because each beat is divided as simply as possible – into two quavers.
Quadruple – because there are four beats in each bar.

If the top number of the time signature is 1, 2, 3 or 4, the piece is in simple time. The piece is also in simple time if the top number is a multiple of 2 but not a multiple of 3.

	simple
duple	2/4 ♫♫
triple	3/4 ♫♫♫
quadruple	4/4 ♫♫♫♫

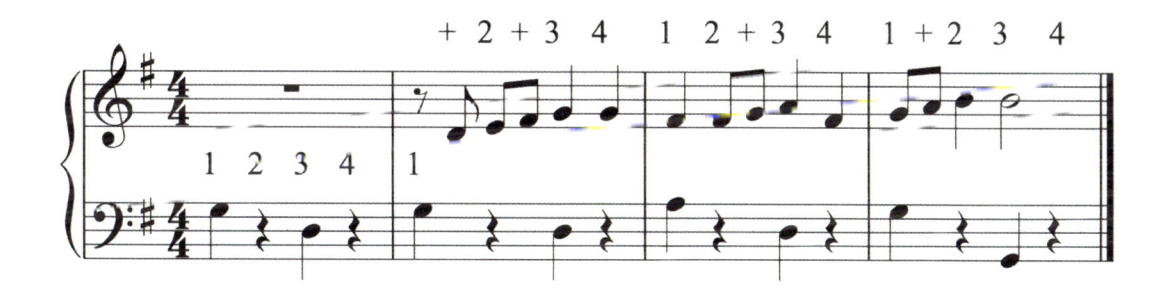

𝄵 Is known as **common time**. It is the same as 4/4

𝄵 is known as **cut common time** or **alla breve**. It is the same as 2/2

At the piano
Look through the pieces that you are learning and check how you should be counting the beats. Improvise a piece in 4/4 and a piece in 3/4 using your chord knowledge.

18 Compound Time Signatures

12/8 - a **compound** time signature – has twelve quavers in each bar. Rather than counting 12 quavers, we count four dotted-crotchet beats per bar.

Count each bar like this: 1-and-a 2-and-a 3-and-a 4-and-a

Compound – because each beat is "compounded" into three quavers.
Quadruple – because there are four dotted-crotchet beats in each bar.

If the top number of the time signature is a multiple of 3 (but not 3 itself), the piece is in compound time.

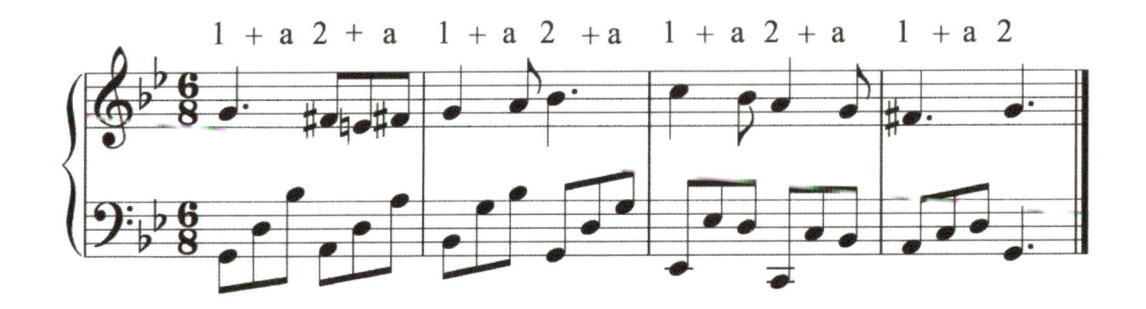

	simple	compound
duple	2/4 ♪♪♪♪	6/8 ♪♪♪ ♪♪♪
triple	3/4 ♪♪♪♪♪♪	9/8 ♪♪♪ ♪♪♪ ♪♪♪
quadruple	4/4 ♪♪♪♪♪♪♪♪	12/8 ♪♪♪ ♪♪♪ ♪♪♪ ♪♪♪

Irregular time signatures have a mix of simple divisions and compound divisions.

5/8 ♪♪♪♪♪   7/8 ♪♪♪♪♪♪♪

At the piano

Look through the pieces that you are learning and check how you should be counting the beats. Improvise a piece in 6/8 and a piece in 9/8 using your chord knowledge.

19 Tuplets

A **tuplet** is an irregular subdivision of the beat into equal portions. The most common kind is the **triplet** where a beat of music in simple time is subdivided into three.

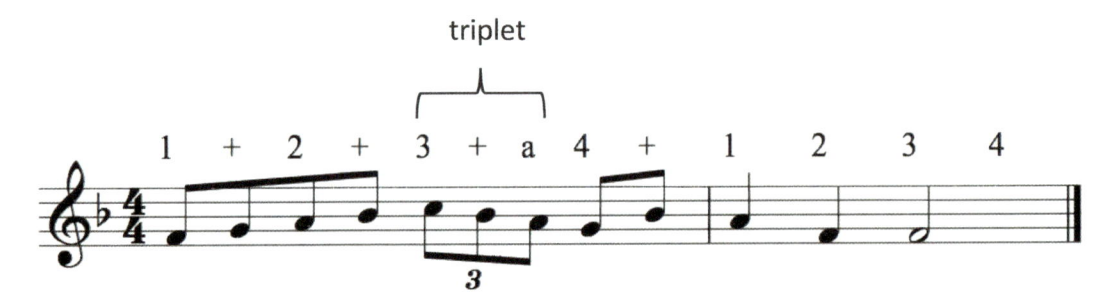

Tuplets can be any irregular number of notes (the regular numbers being 2, 4, 8, 16, 32 etc.).

Tuplets normally result in slightly faster notes.

The exception to this is the **duplet**. A duplet is usually a pair of quavers taking the time of three quavers in compound time.

At the piano

Try to play C major scale with duplets in the left hand and triplets in the right. It's not easy!

3 notes in the time of **2** notes

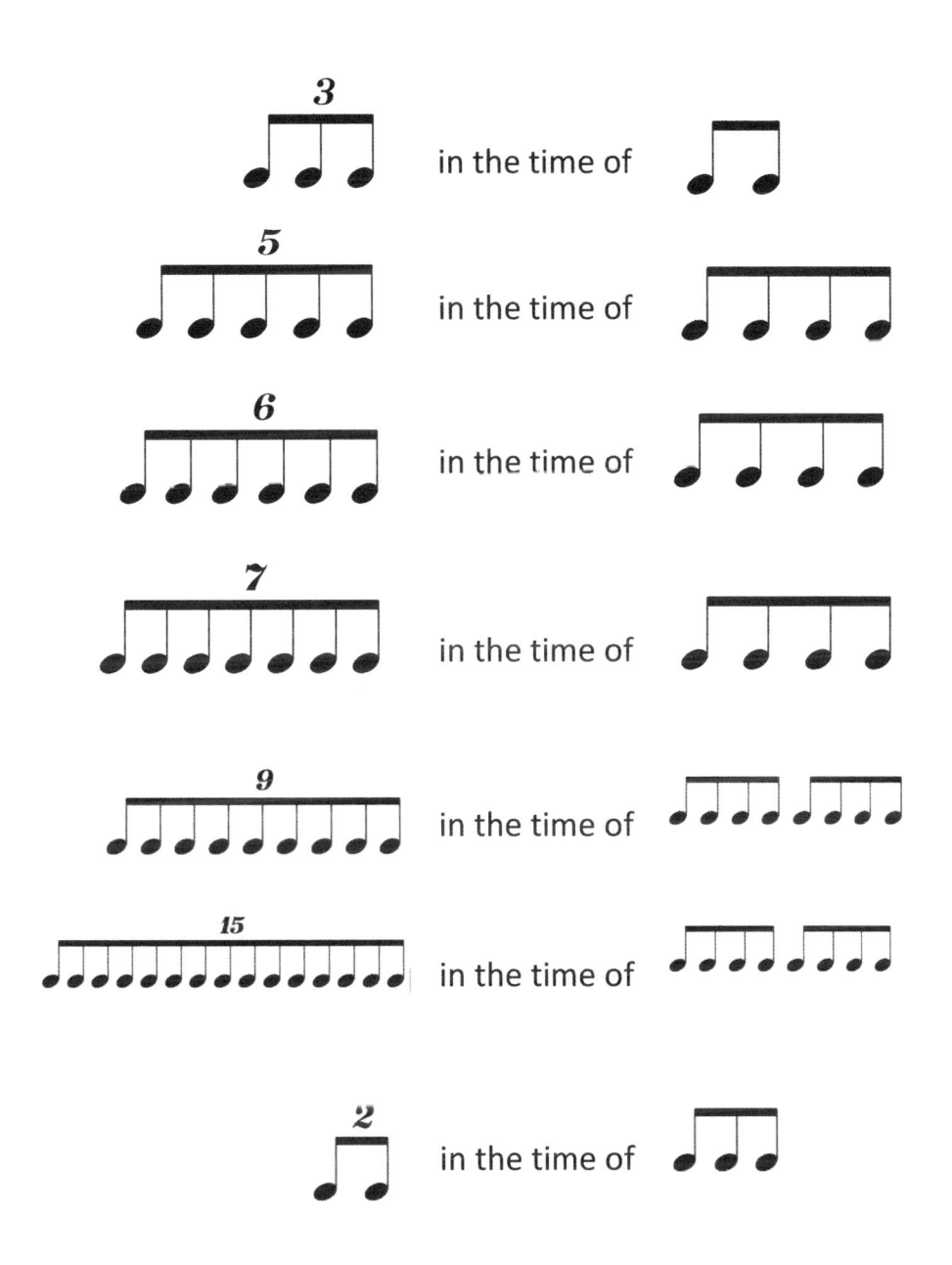

5 notes in the time of **4** notes

6 notes in the time of **4** notes

7 notes in the time of **4** notes

9 notes in the time of **8** notes

15 notes in the time of **8** notes

2 notes in the time of **3** notes

20 Switching Time Signatures

A passage of music in simple time can be rewritten in compound time and vice versa.

The number of beats in the bar must stay the same so for example, a piece of music written in $\frac{2}{4}$ can be rewritten in $\frac{6}{8}$. Both of these time signatures have two beats per bar.

	simple	compound
duple	$\frac{2}{4}$ ♫♫	$\frac{6}{8}$ ♫♫♫♫
triple	$\frac{3}{4}$ ♫♫♫	$\frac{9}{8}$ ♫♫♫♫♫♫
quadruple	$\frac{4}{4}$ ♫♫♫♫	$\frac{12}{8}$ ♫♫♫♫♫♫♫♫

When rewriting a passage, it is essential to understand triplets and duplets and it is a good idea to highlight each beat of the bar before you begin.

To convert a passage of compound time into simple time:

- Consider the number of beats in the bar (duple, triple or quadruple).
- Use the corresponding simple time signature (duple, triple or quadruple).
- Consider each beat in turn. It may be necessary to add triplet signs, to remove duplet signs or to remove dots.

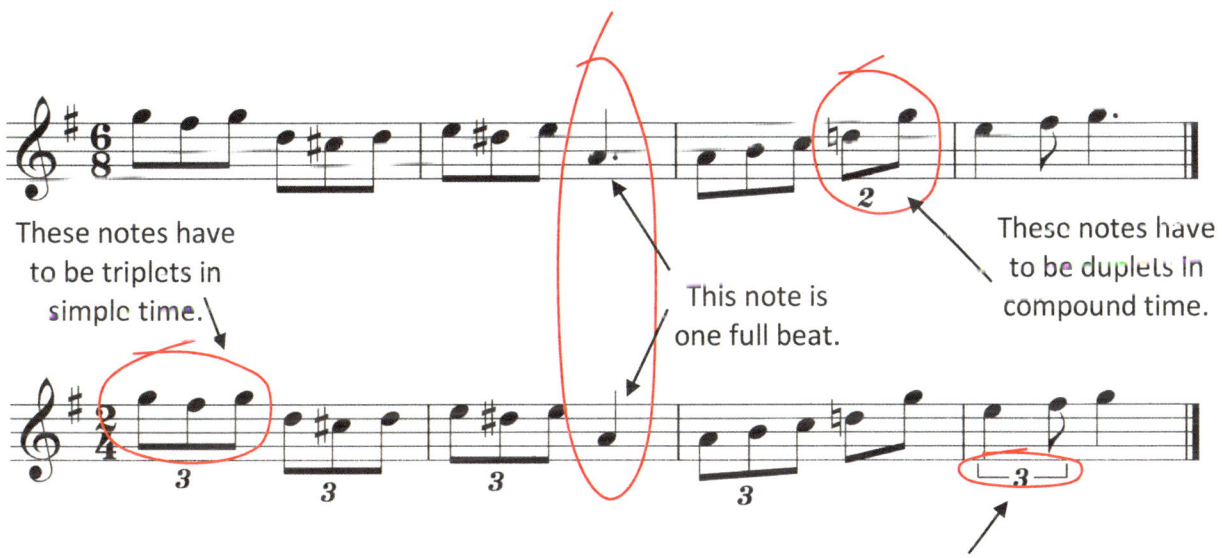

These notes have to be triplets in simple time.

This note is one full beat.

These notes have to be duplets in compound time.

The triplet sign is drawn with a bracket if the notes are not all beamed together.

The lower version, notated in 2/4, has triplet signs in bar 1 to indicate that three quavers should be played in the time of two. The lower version has a normal crotchet in bar 2 rather than a dotted crotchet. The lower version does not need a duplet sign in bar 3.

To convert a passage of simple time into compound time:

- Consider the number of beats in the bar (duple, triple or quadruple).
- Use the corresponding compound time signature (duple, triple or quadruple).
- Consider each beat in turn. It may be necessary to remove triplet signs, to add duplet signs or to add dots.

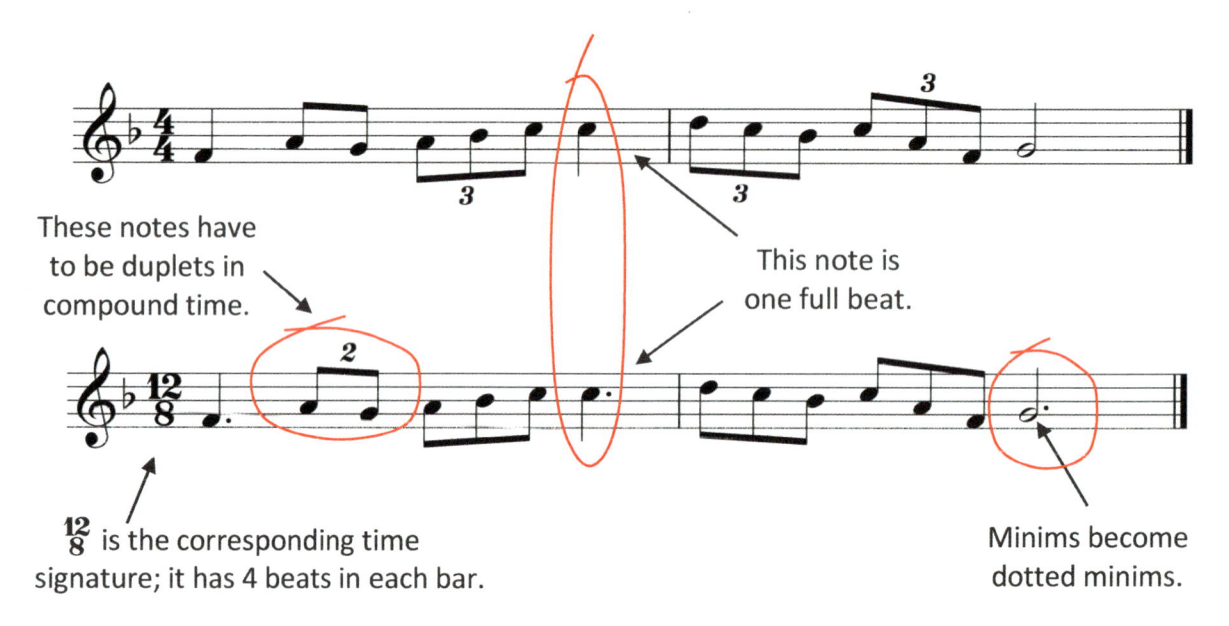

These notes have to be duplets in compound time.

This note is one full beat.

$\frac{12}{8}$ is the corresponding time signature; it has 4 beats in each bar.

Minims become dotted minims.

The lower version, notated in $\frac{12}{8}$, has a duplet in bar 1 to indicate that two quavers are played in the time of three. The lower version has dotted crotchets in bar 1 to indicate notes that are held for a full beat. The lower version has a dotted minim in bar 2 to indicate a note that is held for two full beats.

At the piano

Play through lots of nursery rhymes for example, Humpty Dumpty, Pop goes the Weasel, Ring a ring o' Roses. Work out whether they would be best notated in $\frac{2}{4}$ or $\frac{6}{8}$.

21 Beaming

When notes are **beamed** correctly, it should be easy for the performer to see each beat of the bar.

As a general rule, notes should be beamed in groups of one beat. In simple time signatures, this will often mean that notes are beamed in crotchet groups. In compound time signatures, this will often mean that notes are beamed in dotted crotchet groups.

Occasionally, beams can extend for two beats (four quavers in a row in $\frac{4}{4}$) or even three beats (six quavers in a row in $\frac{3}{4}$).

Note stems can go up or down. The stem goes up if the note is below the middle line of the stave; the stem goes down if the note is on or above the middle line.

When drawing a beamed group of notes, the stems will all go up if most of the notes are below the middle line of the stave; the stems will all go down if most of the notes are above the middle line. The note stems can end up assorted lengths. The beams can be horizontal or, more often, diagonal.

Incorrect version

Ring round crotchet groups

Don't beam across the half bar

Flip stems up

Don't beam across a barline

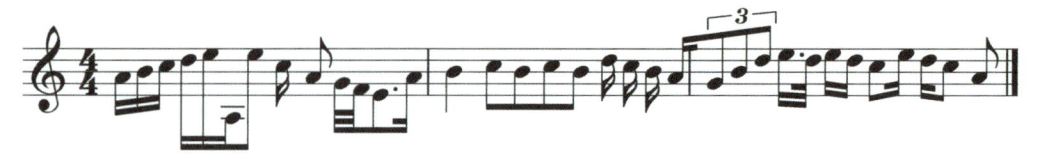

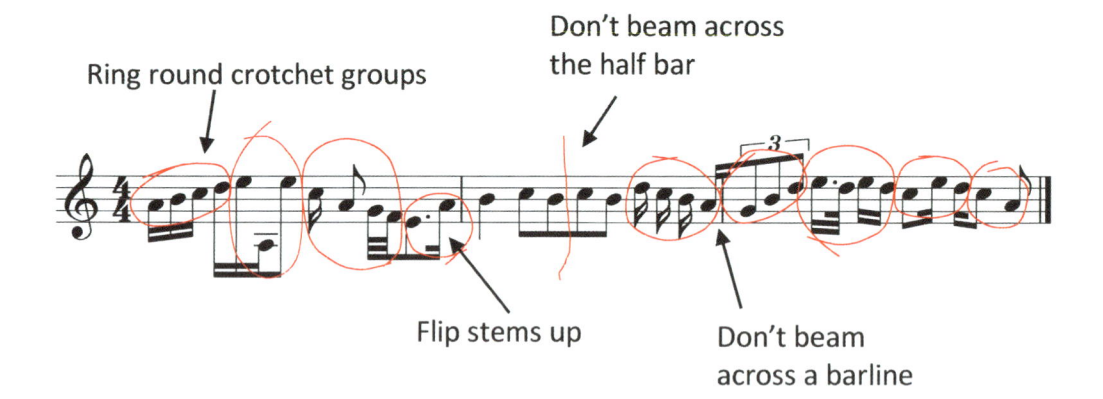

Correct version

The correct version shows each beat clearly. Beat 1 comprises the first four notes, so they are beamed together. Beat 2 comprises the next three notes, so they are beamed together etc.

Some of the note stems have been flipped so that they go up instead of down.

At the piano

Play this melody twice, once reading the incorrect version and once reading the correct version. It should be much easier to read the correct version.

22 Intervals (part 2)

Unisons, 4ths, 5ths and Octaves are known as **perfect** intervals. They are like the pillars of the scales.

2nds, 3rds, 6ths and 7ths can be **major** or **minor**. These intervals give the music a lot of colour and character and are particularly flexible in minor keys.

The major scale comprises perfect intervals and major intervals.

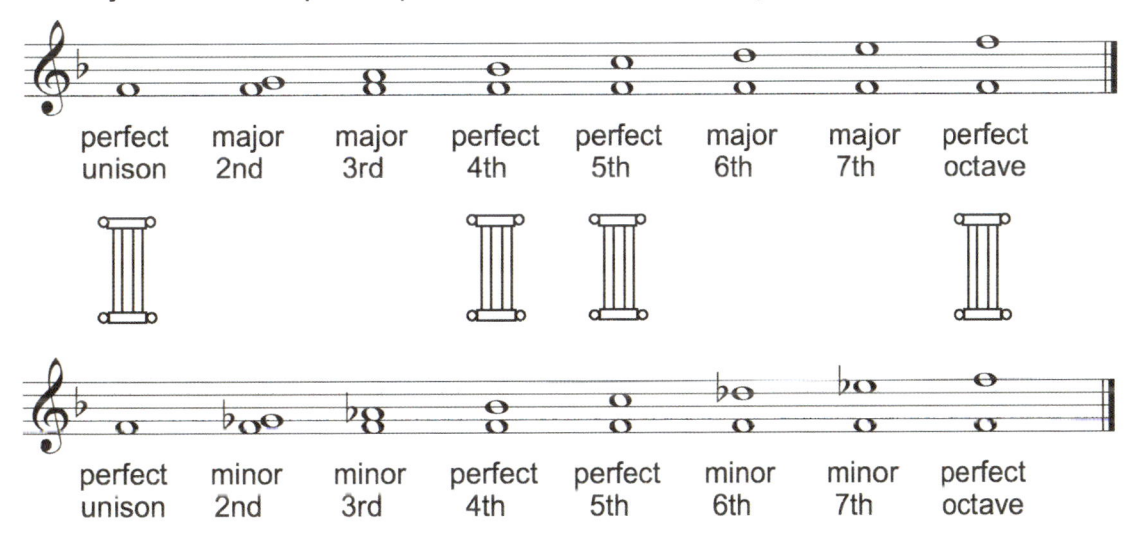

perfect unison — major 2nd — major 3rd — perfect 4th — perfect 5th — major 6th — major 7th — perfect octave

perfect unison — minor 2nd — minor 3rd — perfect 4th — perfect 5th — minor 6th — minor 7th — perfect octave

The minor scale comprises perfect intervals and a mix of major and minor intervals. The particular form of the minor scale shown above (with four minor intervals) is uncommon.

When identifying intervals, it is important to look at the lower note of the interval first. The major scale starting on this lower note determines the major intervals and the perfect intervals.

Major intervals can be changed to minor intervals by flattening the higher note.

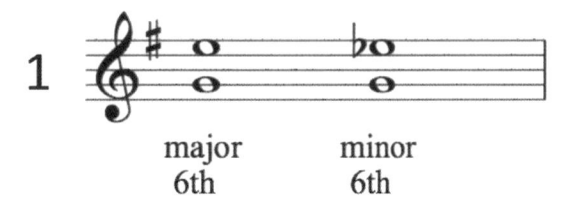

1. In this example, the lower note is G.
The 6th note of G major scale is E.
So, G→E is a major 6th; G→E♭ is a minor 6th.

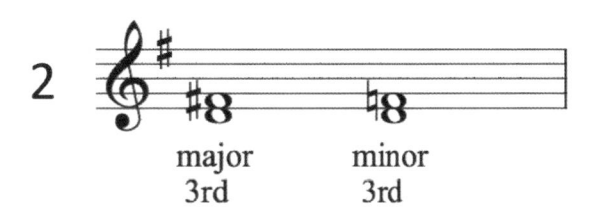

2. In this example, the lower note is D.
The 3rd note of D major scale is F#.
So, D→F# is a major 3rd; D→F is a minor 3rd.

Perfect intervals (Unison, 4th, 5th, 8ve) cannot be converted into minor intervals in this way.

Any interval (perfect or major/minor) can be **augmented** (stretched) or **diminished** (shrunk).

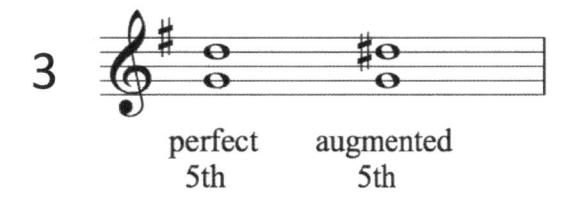

3. In this example, the lower note is G.
The 5th note of G major scale is D.
So, G→D is a perfect 5th; G→D# is an augmented 5th.

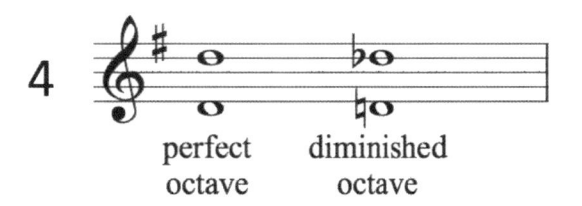

4. In this example, the lower note is D.
The 8th note of D major scale is D.
So, D→D is a perfect 8ve; D→D♭ is a diminished 8ve.

52

To work out the precise quality of an interval:

- Name the two notes of the interval – taking care to look at the key signature and for any accidentals in the same bar.
- Count the letter names (regardless of sharps and flats) from the bottom note to the top, inclusively, to work out the numeric value of the interval.
- Consider the key signature of the **lower** note.
- Compare the printed interval to your expectation of the perfect or major interval constructed on the **lower** note.
- Look at the diagram opposite to see how the printed interval relates to your expectation.

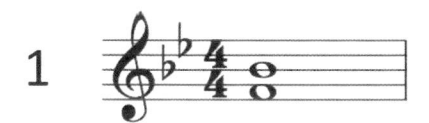

1.
- In this example, the lower note is F; the higher note is B♭.
- The interval is a 4th.
- The scale of F major is F G A B♭ C D E F.
- The 4th note of F major scale is B♭, so this interval is a perfect 4th.

2.
- In this example, the lower note is G♯; the upper note is B.
- The interval is a 3rd.
- There is no scale of G♯ major, so we will consider G major scale - G A B C D E F♯ G.
- The 3rd note of G major scale is B, so G → B is a major 3rd.
- We have a slightly smaller interval G♯ → B, so we have a minor 3rd.

This table shows how the various intervals relate to each other.

Unison 4th 5th 8ve	2nd 3rd 6th 7th
augmented ↑↓ perfect ↑↓ diminished	augmented ↑↓ major ↑↓ minor ↑↓ diminished

One other important piece of vocabulary is the word **compound**. A compound interval is one octave bigger than an ordinary interval.

3

- In this example, the lower note is E♭; the upper note is B♮.
- The interval is an octave plus a 5th.
- The scale of E♭ major is E♭ F G A♭ B♭ C D E♭.
- The 5th note of E♭ major scale is B♭, so E♭ → B♭ is a perfect 5th.
- We have a slightly larger interval E♭ → B♮, so we have an octave plus an augmented 5th.
- We can describe it as a compound augmented 5th.

At the piano

Learn to recognise each of these intervals aurally as well as on the page. Start by memorising the sounds of the 3rd and the 5th, then add a new interval each day.

23 Minor Scales

Minor scales come in three forms – **natural**, **harmonic** and **melodic**.

The natural minor scale is formed simply by writing out the scale with the correct minor key signature. (see Chapter 13)

Example – C natural minor.

The harmonic minor scale has a sharpened 7th. This scale is derived from composers' wanting to use a major chord as the dominant chord for example, E major in the key of A minor (see Chapter 14).

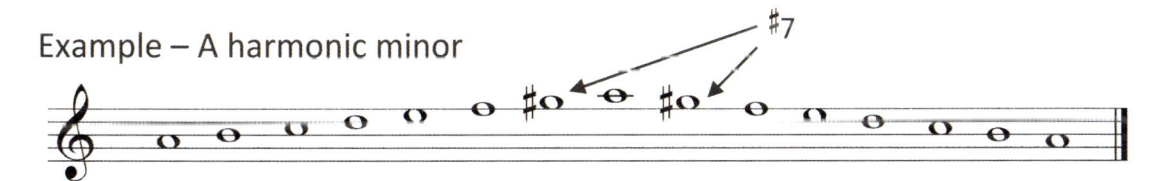

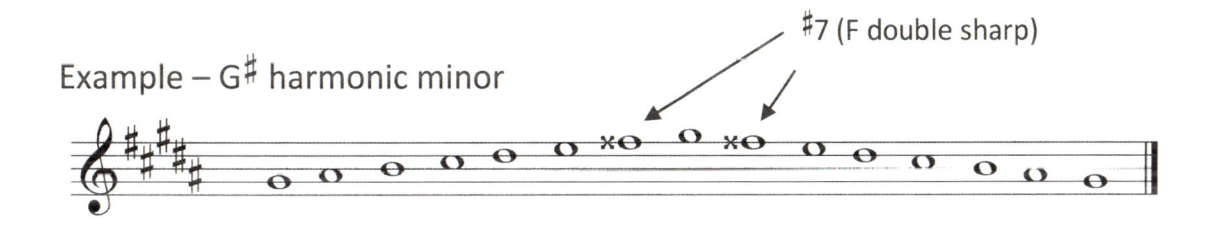

Example – A harmonic minor

♯7

Example – G♯ harmonic minor

♯7 (F double sharp)

The melodic minor scale is based on patterns often found in composers' melodies. It has a sharpened 6th and a sharpened 7th on the way up; it is the same as the natural minor on the way down.

Example – D melodic minor

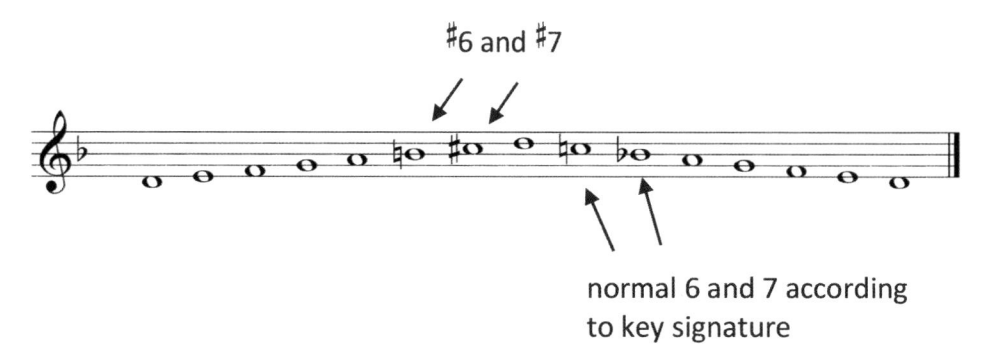

♯6 and ♯7

normal 6 and 7 according to key signature

To construct a minor scale:

- Check the clef that you are using.
- Draw eight consecutive notes starting with the key note (the tonic).
- Look at the inner ring of the Cycle of Fifths to find out how many sharps or flats are necessary in the key signature.
- If the scale needs sharps, use the mnemonic **F**ather **C**hristmas **G**ave **D**ad **A**n **E**lectric **B**lanket to determine which sharps.
- If the scale needs flats, use the mnemonic **B**lanket **E**xploded **A**nd **D**ad **G**ot **C**old **F**eet to determine which flats.
- Draw the sharps and flats next to the applicable notes or as a key signature.
- Sharpen the 6th and 7th degree of the scale as necessary, according to the diagram opposite.

Natural Minor	-
Harmonic Minor	♯7
Melodic Minor ↗	♯6 ♯7
Melodic Minor ↘	-

Sharpening a note is not as simple as adding a ♯ sign. To sharpen a note is to raise it by one semitone – this may involve using a ♯ sign or a ♮ sign.

Flattening a note is not as simple as adding a ♭ sign. To flatten a note is to lower it by one semitone – this may involve using a ♭ sign or a ♮ sign.

At the piano

Take a look at the Cycle of Fifths diagram again. Invent some small melodic fragments using minor scales. Take them on a journey anticlockwise round the Cycle of Fifths.

24 The Chromatic Scale

The **Chromatic Scale** is the scale that comprises every possible note – all the white notes and all the black notes – within the octave.

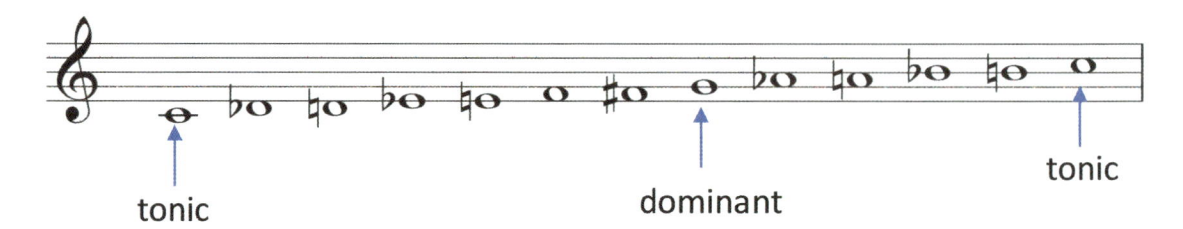

tonic   dominant   tonic

There are various ways to notate the chromatic scale. The version above is the **harmonic chromatic scale**. The easiest way to construct the scale this way is to draw the tonic (1), dominant (5) and tonic (8), then draw each other note twice, then add the necessary accidentals. If the resulting scale is superimposed over a sustained C, it avoids all augmented and diminished intervals apart from the unavoidable F♯.

This is a neat theory but, in practice, composers write the chromatic scale in all sorts of ways. They often use sharps on the way up and flats on the way down. The only golden rule is that there should never be three notes on the same line or space (e.g. D♭, D♮, D♯).

Most music is in a major key or a minor key. When a composer uses fragments of the chromatic scale or even just one note that falls outside the key area, we say that s/he is using **chromaticism**.

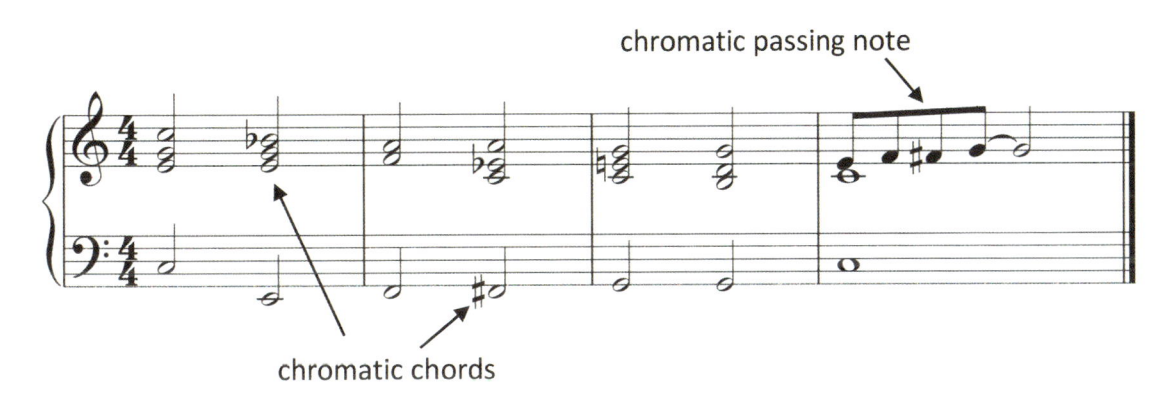

chromatic passing note

chromatic chords

These fleeting chromatic chords do not cause proper modulations. In this example, the passage of music is still in the key of C major. The final cadence (V → I in the key of C) clarifies this.

When you play a chromatic scale on the piano, it is a good idea to play the notes in groups of four, resulting in a 3/4 time feel. Alternatively, you can play in groups of three, resulting in a 12/16 time feel.

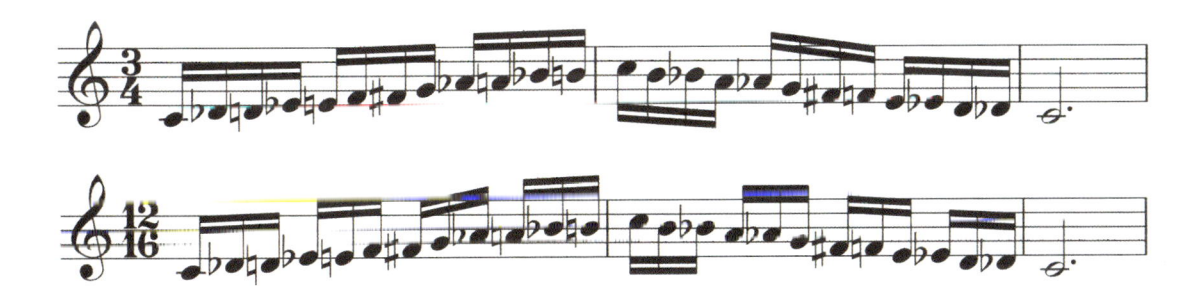

At the piano

Find any four-note chord that you like (F B E A reading from the bottom works well). Move the whole chord up or down a semitone several times.

25 Transposing

Transposing is **changing the key** of a piece of music. The music will sound the same, but will be slightly lower or higher in pitch. Sometimes, singers will change the key of a piece so that it fits better within their range.

Some instruments read their music at **concert pitch** while others read their music in a different key. These other instruments are known as **transposing instruments.** This is a historic anomaly that has advantages as well as some disadvantages.

If a trumpeter plays C it will sound like a B♭, so we say he is playing a Trumpet in B♭. If a Horn player plays C it will sound like an F, so we say he is playing a Horn in F.

To transpose a piece of music:

- Work out the key of the piece (assume it is major).
- Change the key note (the tonic) by the prescribed interval e.g. a major second higher.
- Check, check and double check this interval of transposition.
- Write in the new key signature.
- Notate the piece, moving each note up or down by the prescribed interval. At this stage, ignore any sharps and flats.
- Analyse the sharps, flats and naturals in the original score to work out the **function** of each accidental. Does it raise or lower the pitch?
- Put any necessary sharps, flats and naturals into the new score bearing in mind their function.

Transpose this piece up a minor third.

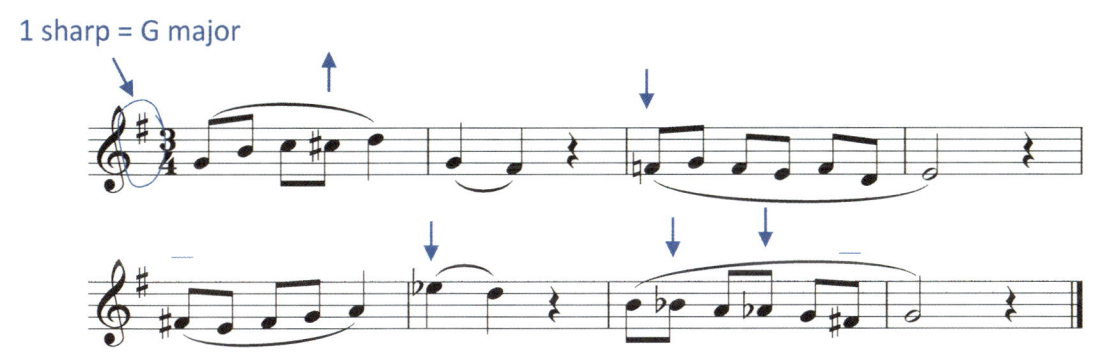

- The original key is G major (one sharp in the key signature).
- The key note is G. The new key note will be a minor third higher (see Chapter 22). The new key note is B♭.
- The new version of the piece will have a key signature of B♭ major (two flats)
- Annotate the G major version of the piece as shown above. ↑ denotes a note that has been sharpened; ↓ denotes a note that has been flattened; — denotes a note that is true to the key signature.
- Make the appropriate adjustments (sharpening and flattening of notes) to the new B♭ major version.

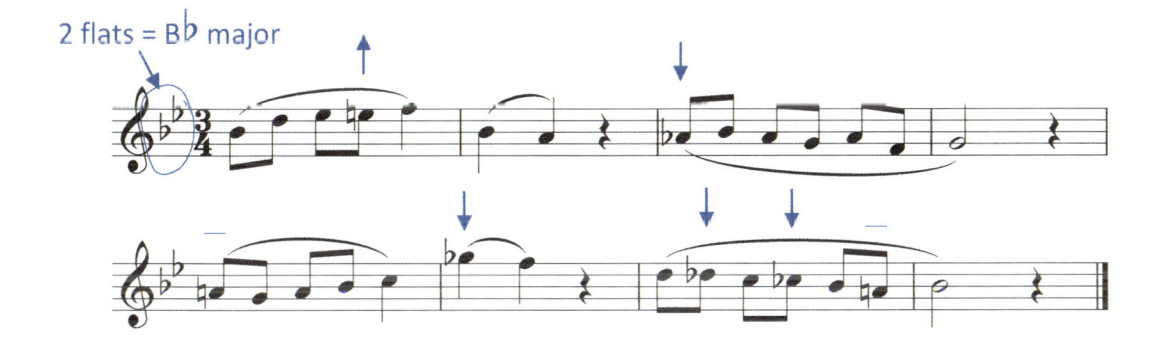

Transpose this piece down a perfect fifth.

- The original key is A major (three sharps in the key signature).
- The new key will be D major – a perfect fifth lower.
- Annotate the A major version of the piece.
- Make the appropriate adjustments to the new D major version.

At the piano

Try some transposing at sight. Start with a piece in C and change it to D major. Remembering the new key signature (two sharps - F and C) will be really important.

26 Ornaments

I have different **ornaments** on my mantelpiece than you and, in fact, different ornaments than I had ten years ago. The same is true of composers' ornaments – they don't always have to be performed the same way.

Ornamentation has always been linked to improvisation. Ornament signs on sheet music were devised as reminders and suggestions to performers. While there is a lot of ambiguity and flexibility in the interpretation of ornaments, there are standard interpretations of each symbol that can be taken as a starting point.

Most ornaments should be performed using notes that are within the key of the piece, whether that results in movement by semitones or tones.

Sometimes there will be small sharps and flats printed above or below an ornament. These indicate that you should play those notes "out of key" accordingly. Working out how to play an ornament is known as "realising" an ornament.

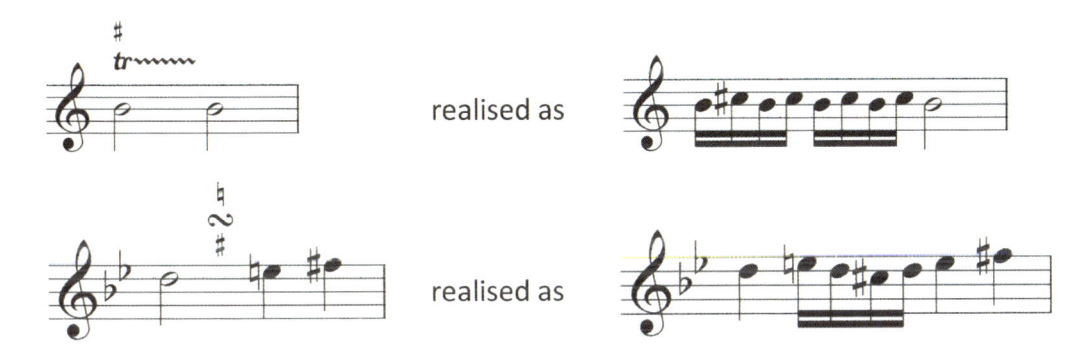

Symbol	Name	Execution
tr~~~~~	trill	(notes)
∿	mordent	(notes)
∿ (lower)	lower mordent	(notes)
∽	turn	(notes)
∽ (inverted)	inverted turn	(notes)
♪♩	appoggiatura	(notes)
♪̸♩	acciaccatura	(notes)

At the piano

Find a piece of music with some ornaments. Work out what those ornaments should be according to the diagram opposite. Now compare this interpretation with recordings of the piece.

27 General Knowledge

Musical instruments are grouped in families. The instruments of the orchestra are classed as **strings**, **woodwind**, **brass** and **percussion**.

Mechanised instruments like the piano and the organ are harder to classify so we often call them **keyboard** instruments.

Note that the saxophone is a woodwind instrument because, although it is made of brass, it produces its sound with a reed much like the clarinet.

The General Knowledge tables opposite show the instruments of each family and indicate what clefs they usually read.

Some of the woodwind and brass instruments are **transposing** instruments. Tenor and Baritone voices read music printed in the treble clef, but they sound one octave lower. The treble clef with the small 8 under it is known as an Octave-treble clef or treble-8 clef. It is also found in guitar music.

At the piano

Play through a piano piece while thinking about what instruments might play each melody and each part of the texture. How might the composer orchestrate the piece?

Orchestral Instruments and Voices

	Strings	Woodwind	Brass	Voices
highest sounding	Violin (treble clef)	Flute (treble clef)	Trumpet in B♭ (treble clef)	Soprano (treble clef)
	Viola (alto clef) (alto)	Oboe (treble clef)	Horn in F (treble clef)	Alto (Contralto) (treble clef)
	'Cello (bass and tenor clef) (tenor)	Clarinet in B♭ (treble clef)	Trombone (bass and tenor clef) (tenor)	Tenor (treble clef 8vb)
lowest sounding	Double Bass (bass clef)	Bassoon (bass and tenor clef) (tenor)	Tuba (bass clef)	Bass (bass clef)

Additional Instruments

	Strings	Woodwind	Keyboard	Voices
	Harp (treble and bass clef)	Saxophone in E♭ or B♭ (treble clef)	Piano (treble and bass clef)	Mezzosoprano (treble clef)
	Guitar (treble clef 8vb)		Organ (treble, bass and bass clef)	Baritone (treble clef 8vb or bass clef)

Tuned Percussion	Untuned Percussion
Notes of definite pitch	**Notes of indefinite pitch**
Timpani, Xylophone, Glockenspiel, Marimba, Celeste, Vibraphone, Tubular Bells	Snare Drum, Bass Drum, Cymbal, Gong, Tambourine, Triangle, Castanet

28 Style

While not strictly a music theory topic, an appreciation of musical **style** is important for understanding composers and their repertoire.

The table opposite necessarily contains some sweeping generalisations, but should provide some insight into musical style and some useful vocabulary to describe music from the various eras. Some of the ideas (counterpoint, terraced dynamics, blue notes) may be new to you. It is worth looking up the meaning of these phrases or, even better, discussing them with your piano teacher.

All the characteristics noted here relate to piano music. This is because music exam candidates are often asked to identify the musical style of a piece played on the piano.

The style of orchestral music, chamber music and vocal music evolved over the same period and is well worth separate study.

At the piano
It is always good to play a variety of music from each era. See if you can find five short pieces, one from each era.

	Baroque	Classical	Romantic	Modern (classical)	Modern (jazzy)
Melody	Continuous semiquavers, long phrases without breaths	Variety, 4-bar phrases	Long phrases that stretch beyond expectations	Angular	Clear phrases, unexpected accents
Harmony	Resultant from the counterpoint, but great variety	I, IV and V	Chromatic chords	Dissonance	Based on ii, IV and V with chromatic alterations
Texture	Counterpoint	Melody plus accompaniment	Full range of the piano	Variety	Very clear melody and bass line
Dynamics	Terraced, often at performer's discretion	Variety	Great variety, often giving character	Variety	Variety, often quite loud
Articulation	Detached	Clear contrasts	Legato pedalling	Often percussive	Great variety, imitating jazz instruments
Ornaments	Many trills and mordents	Occasional trills and turns	Arpeggiation, some long trills and other flourishes	Not so many	Acciaccaturas emulating blue notes.

29 Musical Terms

There are hundreds of musical **terms** to learn for Grade 5 theory exams. On page 70, you will find some of the most common terms presented in a table in the four most-used European languages.

Note that the words for slow all start with the slow letter L; the words for medium start with M and the words for fast can all be said aloud quite fast.

Tempo markings are printed in bold above the staves. Expression markings are usually printed in italics between the treble and bass staves.

The technical names for the **degrees of the scale** are used infrequently, with the exception of tonic and dominant. Remember that the 3rd is the middle (the mediant) of Chord I and the 5th is the other important (dominant) note of the Chord. Like a mirror image, the submediant is a 3rd below the tonic; the subdominant is a 5th below the tonic.

Overleaf, on page 72, you will find a complete list of all the vocabulary needed for ABRSM Grade 5 theory exams. Thanks to Hannah Vitacolonna for providing the nuanced translations (printed in blue).

At the piano

Find one of your piano pieces and make sure you know every instruction. If there are any words or symbols that you don't understand – look them up!

English	Italian	German	French
slow	lento, largo	langsam	lent
medium	moderato	mässig	modéré
fast	allegro	schnell	vite
lively	vivace	lebhaft	vif, anime
slow down	rallentando		cédez
speed Up	accelerando	bewegt	en animant
more	più	mehr	plus
less	meno		moins

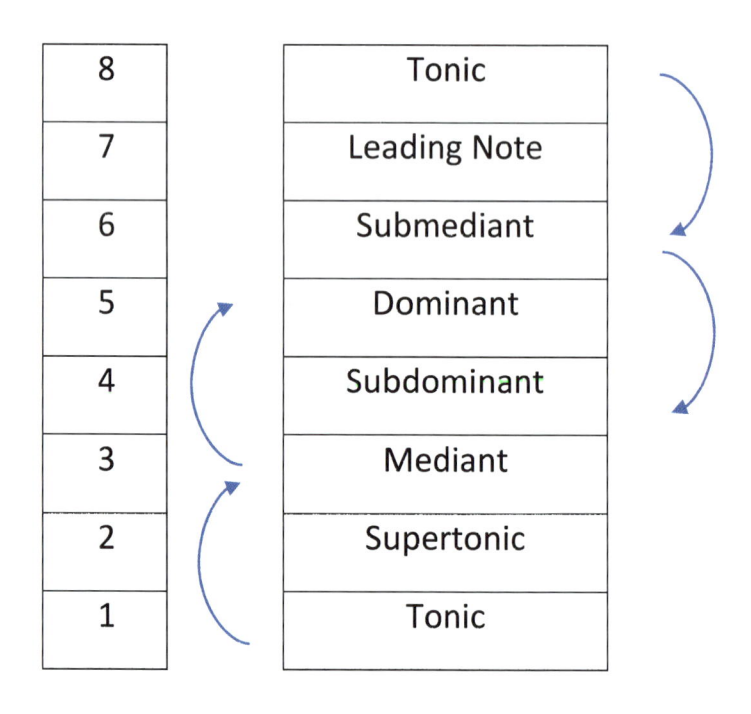

8	Tonic
7	Leading Note
6	Submediant
5	Dominant
4	Subdominant
3	Mediant
2	Supertonic
1	Tonic

" I have added some notes mainly from a linguistic point of view to enlighten students on some of the subtleties and nuances of some of these terms - some of which have very similar meanings to others. It is important to learn the basic meanings of the words for music theory but a better understanding of these terms will also help you play/sing music. As musicians, once we have learned the vocabulary and mastered a piece of music from a technical point of view, we then need to work on different ways of applying the composer's indications and instructions putting our own emotion and expression into the music. It is fun experimenting and worth it. It is all about how we convey emotion and touch the listener. Hopefully a better understanding of the vocabulary will enable you to do this better. "

– Hannah Vitacolonna

Grade 1

a tempo in time

accelerando (or accel.) gradually getting quicker

adagio slow
- with great expression. If you spoke *adagio*, you would be speaking slowly so that you are understood. It also means carefully/calmly/gently/softly/in an unhurried way - as if you don't want to wake a sleeping baby or cause damage or noise.

allegretto fairly quick (but not as quick as allegro)

allegro fast

andante at a medium ("walking") speed
- moving at a walking pace

cantabile in a singing style
- It literally means singable/something that can be sung.

crescendo (or cresc.) gradually getting louder
- In Italian, this literally means to swell/surge/grow in intensity.

da capo (or D.C.) repeat from the beginning

decrescendo (or decresc.) gradually getting quieter
- This often follows a crescendo/a passage of increased loudness. It is the opposite of *increase* and literally means to decrease/lessen/decline.

diminuendo (or dim.) gradually getting quieter
- This can refer to a whole passage of music as opposed to following a *crescendo*. It could also indicate slowing down. It literally means decrease/dwindle/reduce the amount of something.
  Decrescendo and diminuendo can be interchangeable and used together in music. A final diminuendo in a piece could fade to nothing but there may still be additional markings from the composer or publisher to lower the sound and slow it down even more.

dolce — sweet, soft

f (= forte) — loud
- In Italian, this also means strong, determined and intense.

ff (= fortissimo) — very loud

fine — the end

legato — smoothly
- literally to play the notes with no pauses. It comes from the Italian verb *legare* which means to bind/tie/connect together.

mf (= mezzo forte) — moderately loud (literally "half loud")

moderato — moderately (allegro moderato: moderately quick)
- in a measured way

mp (= mezzo piano) — moderately quiet (literally "half quiet")

p (= piano) — quiet
- also means soft/delicately/slowly/hushed in Italian

pp (= pianissimo) — very quiet

rallentando (or rall.) — gradually getting slower
- In Italian, this translates as slow down/reduce speed (in a car you would brake).

ritardando (or ritard. or rit.) — gradually getting slower
- This literally means to delay/be late.

staccato (or stacc.) — detached
- separate notes. All the notes should be broken off from the rest.

◁ — crescendo (gradually getting louder)

▷ — diminuendo (gradually getting quieter)

⌒ — over two different notes (not to be confused with a tie) or over a group of notes is called a "slur"; perform the notes smoothly

8va ⌐¯¯¯¯¯¯¯¯¯¯¬	(over a not or notes): perform an octave higher
8vb ⌐_____⌐	(under a note or notes): perform an octave lower
.	a dot over or under a note = staccato
>	over or under a note = accent
⌒	pause on the note
M.M. = 72	72 crotchet beats in a minute
(or just ♩ = 72)	(M.M. is short for Maelzel's metronome)

Grade 2

alla marcia in the style of a march

allargando broadening (getting a little slower and probably a little louder
- This literally means to widen/stretch out.

con moto with movement

con, col with

dal segno (or D.S.) repeat from the sign 𝄋

e, ed and

espressivo (or espress. or espr.) expressive

fp (= fortepiano) loud, then immediately soft

grave very slow, solemn
- serious/sombre

grazioso graceful
- also means refined/delicate/pretty

largo slow

lento slow

ma but

meno less

molto very, much

mosso, moto	movement (meno mosso: slower; con moto: with movement)

- *mosso* is the past participle of the verb *to move*. It is used to describe a rough sea/wavy hair/a blurry photo (the camera moved). Both convey a sense of motion/shakiness/the opposite of still and calm.

non troppo	not too much
più	more
poco	a little
presto	fast (faster than allegro)

- rapidly and up tempo. In Italian, this word also means "early".

ritenuto (or riten. or rit.)	held back

- This literally means to retain/constrain/hold back.

senza	without
vivace, vivo	lively, quick
⌢ ⋅ ⋅ ⋅	means that the notes should be slightly separated (semi-staccato) but less so than notes with ordinary staccato dots
▼	indicates a super-staccato (staccatissimo): the note is to be played as briefly as possible and perhaps accented as well
—	means that the note is to be given a slight pressure (and generally slightly separated) = tenuto

Grade 3

agitato   agitated
- indicates "play quickly with agitation or excitement ". In Italian, a person described as agitato would be shaken or upset. It also means rough (the sea)/shaken/stirred/mixed (in cooking).

andantino   slightly faster than andante (but may also mean slightly slower)
- In Italian andante means *at a walking pace*. It comes from the verb *andare* - to go and indicates movement/going somewhere. *Andantino* in musical terms is usually lighter and quicker than *andante*. Although andantino is the diminutive form of andante and should indicate a slower tempo than andante, it actually came to mean the opposite.

animato   animated, lively (animando: becoming more lively)

ben   well

con forza   with force
- also means vigour/strength/energy

energico   energetic

giocoso   playful, merry
- jolly/fun

legglero   light, nimble
- graceful

maestoso   majestic
- grandiose

marcato, marc.   emphatic, accented
- pronounced

pesante   heavy
- with weight/importance/forceful - play impressively. The opposite of delicate.

prestissimo   very fast

prima, primo   first

risoluto   bold, strong
- determined/tenacious/steadfast

scherzando   playful, joking
- jestful

semplice   simple, plain
- basic

sempre   always

sf, sfz, sforzando, sforzato)   forced, accented
- can also mean "strained" in Italian

simile (or sim.)   in the same way
- alike/similar

sostenuto, sost.   sustained
- may imply a slowing of tempo too. It is the past participle of the verb *sostenere* which means to support/hold up/maintain. In musical terms, it means sustained to, or beyond, a note's full value. It can refer to a whole movement or passage where the notes are prolonged.

subito, sub.   suddenly

tranquillo   calm
- relaxed, tranquil

triste, tristamente   sad, sorrowful
- melancholy

Grade 4

affetuoso   tenderly
- with affection

alla breve   with a minim beat, equivalent to, implying a faster tempo than the note values might otherwise suggest
- This literally means "on the breve (a half-note)". Also known as "cut time". When a musician sees this he/she should play notes more cleanly with slightly shorter length. This indication is often used in military marches.

amabile   amiable, pleasant
- play in a charming, gracious manner

appassionato   with passion

assai   very (allegro assai: very quick)

come prima   as before

comodo   convenient (tempo comodo: at a comfortable speed)
- at leisure. This also translates as comfort/convenient/cushy.

con brio   con brio: with vigour, lively
- with vivacity, zest and oomph (colloquial)

deciso   with determination
- resolved/confident

larghetto   rather slow (but not as slow as largo)
- slower than andante, but not as slow as largo

mesto   sad
- miserable/dejected/with melancholy

misterioso   mysteriously

ritmico   rhythmically

rubato, tempo rubato   with some freedom of time

stringendo   gradually getting faster
- from the verb *stringere* which means to squeeze/press/grip/tighten. Accelerate the tempo and gradually press forward.

animé   animated, lively

douce   sweet

lent   slow

modéré   at a moderate speed

retenu   held back (en retenant: holding back, slowing a little)

vite   quick

Grade 5

a niente — to nothing

ad libitum, ad lib. — at choice, meaning that a passage may be played freely

attacca — go straight on to the next section of music
- from the Italian verb *attacare* - to attach/stick two or more things together

cantando — singing

con dolore — with grief
- also means heartache/pain/suffering/sorrow

con spirito — with spirit

doloroso — sorrowful

largamente — broadly
- A slow, broad tempo, keeping beats far apart from one another

morendo — dying away
- of tone and slowing of movement

perdendosi — dying away
- literally losing itself/oneself

quasi — as if, resembling

rinforzando, rf, rfz — reinforcing
- also strengthen, bolster

smorzando, smorz. — dying away in tone and speed
- In Italian, this verb, *smorzare*, literally means to soften/deaden/muffle.

sonoro — resonant, with rich tone
- Literally "voiced", resounding/sonorous/grandiose. Giving out a deep resonant sound.

sotto voce	in an undertone
- below the voice	
langsam	slow
lebhaft	lively
mässig	at a moderate speed
ruhig	peaceful
schnell	fast
traurig	sad

Italian terms that refer to specific instruments

Strings and Brass	***con sordini***	with mutes
	senza sordini	without mutes
Strings	***arco***	play with the bow (a direction after pizzicato)
	V	an "up bow"
	⊓	a "down bow"
	⌒	a slur means the notes should be played in one stroke of the bow (up or down)
	pizzicato	plucked
	sul G	play on the G string
	sul ponticello	play near the bridge
Piano	***una corda***	press the left pedal (literally "one string")
	tre corde	release the left pedal (literally "three strings")
	𝄢𝄽. _____	press/release the right pedal
	〰	spread the notes of a chord quickly, starting from the bottom note

30 History of Music Theory

The oldest instrument that has been discovered is an ivory flute made about 40,000 years ago. But humans had voices and were using stone tools well before this date, so it is safe to assume that our ancestors have been making music for many years. We don't know if the songs they sang and the melodies they played bore any relation to any music we know now.

China
The Lü shih ch'un ch'iu is an important Chinese text written around 250 BC. It contains the myth of Ling Lun who found that bamboo flutes cut in mathematical proportions made pleasing sounds. A flute that plays C – when you cut a third of its length off – will play G. By this method, he formulated six notes of the male Phoenix (going up in 5ths) and six notes of the female phoenix (going down in 5ths). These notes equate to the twelve notes of our chromatic scale and/or Cycle of Fifths. Ling Lun was alive at the time of the Yellow Emperor, nearly 3000 BC.

India
Indian musicians also recognise the importance of the fifth, but they are interested in the immense variety of melodies, mood and colours that can be produced with great flexibility of the notes in between. Indian musicians use a system known as Sargam which is similar to sol-fa notation. Sargam was in use by at least 200 BC. The Natya Shastra, written by Bharata Muni, is a text that is approximately 2000 years old. It contains chapters on music that describe the octave divided into 22 srutis (microtones).

Europe

The Ancient Greeks, and likely the Babylonians and Sumerians before them, were aware that a chain of perfect fifths - F C G D A E B results in the diatonic scale - C D E F G A B C. Around 340 BC, Aristoxenus, a follower of Aristotle and the Peripatetic School, wrote a treatise on music where he advocated using the ear to tune intervals rather than the mathematical principles of the earlier Pythagorean school.

Western Europeans devised the modern notation system during the course of the 9th to the 17th century. Initially used as a memory-aid for singing plain chant melodies, notation became the chief method of transmitting musical ideas until the advent of recording and digital technology in the 20th century.

Certain European composers have written such highly-crafted and beautiful music that their compositional styles and techniques are studied by other composers and students. A typical course of study would include the masses and motets of Palestrina, the chorales of JS Bach, the string quartets of Haydn and the song accompaniments of Schubert and Schumann.

Jazz

Jazz evolved in America in the twentieth century. The style is an inextricable mix of European, African and authentically American ideas. Contemporary jazz musicians need an excellent knowledge of theory in order to create complex music spontaneously. Dizzy Gillespie famously codified the language of bebop in the 1940s; George Russell wrote an influential jazz theory book in 1953. Jazz musicians practise patterns around the Cycle of Fifths habitually and this helps them to develop their skills of improvisation.

Printed in Great Britain
by Amazon